STEP
BY
STEP

STEP
⟢ BY ⟣
STEP

A Memoir of Hope,
Friendship, Perseverance,
and Living the
American Dream

BERTIE
BOWMAN

ONE WORLD
BALLANTINE BOOKS / NEW YORK

Published in the United States by One World Books,
an imprint of The Random House Publishing Group,
a division of Random House, Inc., New York.

ONE WORLD is a registered trademark and the One World colophon
is a trademark of Random House, Inc.

Library of Congress Cataloging-in-Publication Data
Bowman, Bertie.
Step by step : a memoir of hope, friendship, perseverance,
and living the American dream / Bertie Bowman.
p.   cm.
ISBN 978-0-345-50411-1 (hardcover : alk. paper)
1. Bowman, Bertie, 1931–   2. Bowman, Bertie, 1931—Childhood and youth.
3. African Americans—Biography.   4. United States. Congress. Senate. Committee on
Foreign Relations—Officials and employees—Biography.   5. African American
businesspeople—Washington (D.C.)—Biography.   6. Civic leaders—Washington
(D.C.)—Biography.   7. Washington (D.C.)—Biography.   8. Summerton (S.C.)—
Biography.   9. Summerton (S.C.)—Race relations.   10. African Americans—
Segregation—South Carolina—History—20th century.   I. Title.
E185.97.B78A3 2008
328.73'092—dc22
[B]
2008000322

Printed in the United States of America

www.oneworldbooks.net

246897531

First Edition

Book design by Susan Turner

To my wife, Elaine, who has made all the difference in my life, and to the "downstairs employees" who made all the difference in the life of the United States Capitol.

⟨ FOREWORD ⟩
by President Bill Clinton

I first met Bertie Bowman more than forty years ago. I was a young, eager junior at Georgetown University, excited to begin my job on Capitol Hill as assistant clerk on the U.S. Senate Foreign Relations Committee. Bertie was the full-time assistant to the Committee's documents clerk, and the only African American on the Senate Foreign Relations Committee staff. He was exactly the kind of person you want to be spending a lot of time with when you are a 20-year-old, fifth-generation Arkansan embarking on his first Capitol Hill adventure— kind, bighearted, generous with his time and friendship, knowledgeable, and dedicated. He also had an amazing life story: At age thirteen, he ran away from his Summerton, South Carolina, home, which he shared with his thirteen siblings, to our nation's capitol to take his Senator up on his offer to "drop by and see me," as Bertie had heard him tell an all-white crowd. He had worked his way up from sweeping the Capitol steps to become a member of the Foreign Relations Committee staff by the time I met him. Bertie and I have remained in touch since then, and I am proud to call him my friend.

With *Step by Step: A Memoir of Hope, Friendship, Perseverance, and Living the American Dream,* readers will see firsthand why I love Bertie Bowman so much. From his humble beginnings as a poor farm boy in the segregated South to his years as a junior member of the Senate janitorial staff to his tenure as hearing coordinator for the Senate Foreign Relations Committee, he epitomizes the kind of citizen that makes this country great; he also is representative of the kind of employee who ensures the smooth operation of our federal government. Folks like Bertie don't make the newspapers, and the American people usually will never know their names, but they work hard every day to get done all the things the people in the papers get credit for. *Step by Step* is lively, personal, heartbreaking at times and heartwarming at others, but always inspiring, and a refreshing antidote to the negativity that permeates so much of what is written about Washington.

Bertie is living proof of why it is both morally right and in our country's best interest to embrace the talents and gifts of all our people, regardless of race, educational background, or station in life. Most important, *Step by Step* truly is, as its title indicates, a testament to the power and promise of the American Dream: the idea that if we work hard, play by the rules, help others, and believe in ourselves and our country, we can accomplish great things.

CONTENTS

TEN

STEP
BY
STEP

❯❯❯ ONE ❮❮❮

Summerton, South Carolina

A S A RESULT OF HAPHAZARD RECORD KEEPING, I STARTED OUT LIFE with two "official" birthdays, but not much else. Legend has it that in the early 1930s down in Summerton, South Carolina, a midwife named "Mrs. Jessie" rode around Clarendon County in an old buggy pulled by a white horse. The horse was reliable, knew the roads by heart, and took her to the farms of the colored families. Mrs. Jessie delivered all of the colored babies, and I was no exception. I was born in 1931.

Local people still share tales today about the lady with the white horse. The elders say Mrs. Jessie would hitch her horse outside the courthouse door, strut past the onlookers, and enter, waving a long list of kids' names for all to see.

"Here they is!" Mrs. Jessie would proudly proclaim. "Here's all the babies I brung into the world since I seen you last!"

The clerks permitted Mrs. Jessie to put the names into the record book herself, using her jagged scrawl on the pages to list the health, weight, and other physical descriptions of the baby. That was a big honor for a colored person. Nobody was allowed to touch the record book unless they were white. When Mrs. Jessie came to my entry, the comment listed beside my name, Bertie Herbert Bowman, was in big letters: "WATE—MUCH AS 10 BAG FLOWER—LONG LIKE DADDY ARM."

The courthouse ledger showed my birthday on May 5, 1931. In her usual state of frenzy and haste, Mrs. Jessie recorded thirty-two other births, but obviously she did not midwife all those babies in one day. She might have been a legend with a constitution of iron, but she wasn't superhuman.

In Summerton, a hamlet of nearly 2,000 people at the time, important events were always noted in the family Bible. Since Mrs. Jessie often possessed the sole responsibility for making the critical notations in the Bibles, many families still have her printed comments in their holy books. Sadly, our family Bible burned, so I have no way of knowing what was written inside, but I do recall that Mrs. Jessie's penmanship in it was a direct match to that in the county record book.

I would later learn from my father's cousin Celestine Gregory that my birthdate was not May 5 but April 12, a fact of which she was certain because I was born on the same day as her brother, Billy Nelson.

I was the fifth child, my father's fourth son in a family that would eventually grow to include fourteen children. My father's side of the family originally came from Bertie County in North Carolina, which may provide a clue as to the origin of my first name.

Mary Ragin was my mother's maiden name. I was told that she was uncommonly beautiful. My mother, with her glowing brown skin and her Indian-black straight hair, drew stares from men and women alike when she walked down the street. I don't remember her too well. She died when I was little, her heart stopping suddenly in a difficult childbirth. I don't remember how old she was when she died because I was so young.

MY FATHER, ROBERT BOWMAN, took another wife, Mary Rosa Richardson, a woman, like my mother, of strength, kindness, and compassion. Our family already had a full complement of children: John, Robert, Bertha, Charlie, and Annie before me, and then my two youngest brothers,

Rufus and Ernest. But now our blended clan included Rosa's children: Charlotte, Larry, Wilhelmenia, Dorothy, and Jimmy Lee, who was adopted by my mother as a baby. My family counts the loss of a girl who lived for only one month as a part of the family as well. Rosa didn't replace my mother in my heart, but she was the woman who mostly raised me, and I loved her. My father made a very wise choice in choosing a mate. In contrast to my father, with his steel will, Rosa made us think that everything was possible and guided our household through some very tough times. She was pretty, with a smooth, fair-skinned complexion, and was unassuming even though she ruled us kids with a soft, firm command. If she couldn't make you obey her just by appealing to your sense of what was right, a well-placed threat would usually do the trick.

Of course, I wasn't perfect as a child. If I did something wrong, she would give me a little smack on the hands. Her discipline wasn't very much at all, compared to my father's. "I'm going to tell your father 'bout you being bad," my mother would warn our group with a stern face. "And you know what he will do to you if you don't do right. He'll heat your rear ends up with a switch and I know you won't like that."

My father laid down the rules to maintain the household, a set of tough regulations that would control a whole brood of youngsters and keep order. We cooperated and never challenged him. If the rule of law had broken down, everything would have dissolved into mayhem, and neither of my parents was going to stand for that foolishness. No back talk was tolerated. Chores were divided by gender. In the early mornings, it was the boys' responsibility to start a fire and keep it going. The girls were not allowed to make fires, but they were permitted to cook and bake. The menu was standard and routine: bacon and eggs or ham and eggs, grits or cornbread and syrup. We had it daily and were glad for it because it filled our bellies. A lot of people around there didn't have that. Sometimes during the winter months we ate mush, which was the same as oatmeal, but consisted of cornmeal.

Mom and Dad loved to take late walks, talking low and giggling, on summer nights when the moon was out shining. We children would sit on the porch and watch them go down the road holding hands, teasing each other, for as far as we could see. We loved to see them like that. Now, don't ask how long they stopped, where they went, or what they did. All I know is that they loved to take walks in the moonlight. Neighbors have since told me that my father was a real romantic. I know he loved his wife and family, but I knew him as a very tough man.

Home was a wooden farmhouse with a tin roof under a big oak tree that still stands today. I hear it is one of the biggest oak trees in all of South Carolina. In our simply constructed house, the bedrooms seemed very big to me during my childhood. The boys had one bedroom, the girls another, and my parents slept in their own bedroom. The girls had a much bigger room because my parents said they needed their privacy. We eight boys, restless and noisy, slept in big iron beds, four to a bed, and when it was cold we covered up with very heavy quilts made by our relatives. We each had our place in the bed, but we had to take turns getting up to put wood on the fire during the chilly night. Sometimes we would huddle in the dark, hands outstretched, warming ourselves near the blaze. Occasionally, one of us would wet the bed. To this day I don't know which boy did it and the culprit has never admitted it. Still, I do know that often when it was my turn to put the log on the fire, I would rise out of a dry spot in the bed and after my departure, my brothers would all roll over. When I returned, I was forced to sleep on the wet spot.

My family was no better situated than everybody else. These were rough times, during the Great Depression, and even white people were suffering. Every black person was in the same boat, trying to eke out a living, keep their family fed, and maintain the land. My family was poor, but we kids did not know how poor we were. We had a kitchen stove that we cooked on, and a potbelly stove we used to burn wood for heat. It could get really cool during those long winter nights. I cannot remember ever sitting around the dinner table talking and eating, because we all couldn't fit because of the sheer number of all of us. In fact, I cannot recall family conversations anyway. The rule in my home was that children talked with children, adults talked with adults, and no breach of the law was tolerated. We were never to talk with grown-ups until some adult asked us a question. And at mealtime we lined up and got our food, then ate it either on the porch in the winter or out in the yard during the summer when the house was too hot.

In the sweltering heat of the summer, nothing could outdo a bath. I remember taking baths underneath the big oak tree, its large branches forming a canopy over the two tin tubs in its dark shadows. Before we went into the field, we put the tubs on the ground and before long, the bright yellow sun had warmed the water into a hot soup. My mother supervised the bath activities, making sure that everybody got a decent share of time. Nobody hogged the bathwater with my mother looking out. There was one tub for the girls and one for the boys, with heaps of fun. My sisters got in and out of the tub quickly, proud and modest, and then we boys would have a good time jumping from tub to tub, splashing and acting a fool.

Winter was the harshest season of all. During the winter months, the wind would whistle through the wooden boards of the house, sending a chill through you if you were not standing directly in front of the fire. The water was cold when it was time to wash up. We didn't take baths in the wintertime. To generate enough heat, we burned oak most of the time to warm the house. We took turns spinning and circling our bodies to take advantage of the glow. It was a rotating kind of warmth.

There was an old saying we all learned as kids: "Do you know why people from South Carolina wear long underwear in the winter and the summer, too?"

"Because what will keep you warm in the winter, will keep you cool in the summer," people used to reply.

In the winter, I worked in the barn, getting the hay and feeding the animals. Everyone in the family shared in the hard work. We had to get ourselves out of bed before dawn every day to do the chores while our parents slept. The rooster would wake us up. We never had an alarm clock and didn't know any people who had clocks in their homes. I didn't even know that clocks had alarms. The only place where I saw a clock was in town.

None of us owned wristwatches either. We told time in different ways, by the angle of the sun and its rays, by the position of the moon in the night sky. We knew it was getting past noon when we felt the temperature rise. We knew the hottest time of the day was from the period of noon to 2 p.m. After that, we told time by how far away the sun was from setting in a shimmer on the horizon. You knew when winter was going to set in, around the first part of December, because you would see a beautiful full moon come up in a silver glow just after sunset. Coming from a farming background, people were close to nature and its season. Everybody paid close attention to the wishes and demands of the earth. Not so today.

In the still of the night, you would have all kinds of sounds coming from the woods, but you usually didn't know what animals or things were making the sounds. Creatures of the dark. Night was a very happy time for me, since I could just look up into the sky and dream about somewhere else.

After the morning chores were completed, we'd walk a tiring three miles to school, while the white children, in buses, passed us on the road to their well-equipped classrooms and modern textbooks. Some of the black parents hated the bright-yellow school buses that were packed with the white children who cruelly waved to us as we trudged over the dirt roads. Many of the school officials said blacks did not pay enough taxes or show enough interest in quality education, so such luxuries or conveniences were not budgeted for the black schools.

Officials called this type of school system "separate but equal," which was part and parcel of the Jim Crow process. As a southern black farm boy, I did not look at Jim Crow as oppressive; it was a way of life that I was raised in and in whose grip I probably would die. Every black person tolerated its isolation, its hatred, its way of regarding colored people as inferiors. When I was young, I and the other black kids walked to school with sore feet and dusty clothes to the building in St. Paul many miles away from home. Sometimes we could catch a ride in a wagon pulled by mules or, if we were lucky, a black farmer would drive us in the truck owned by the white boss.

In one of my best school memories in the early grades, I was eager to be cast for the school play, "Little Red Riding Hood," and got the part of the "Big Bad Wolf" character. I loved acting. During the rehearsals, I proceeded to huff and puff but nothing much came out because I could not stop laughing. Following a few rehearsals where I continued to laugh nonstop, my teacher, Mrs. Blackwell, concluded that I was not good for the part. She did not like my clowning around. Instead, she permitted me to sing "God Bless America" before the start of the play. I did all right. At least, no one laughed.

My favorite thing to do at lunchtime was to play marbles. With the one-room schoolhouse in the background, we would all stand in circles in the rocky yard, hunched over and propelling the marbles against one another. The gang was all there, the little kids in one corner, the medium kids in another, and the bigger kids in a prized area. I was very good at this game and used to win all of the marbles.

One day, when I was deep into playing, I placed the marbles in a bag and some of the older boys approached me from behind and snatched it. I was so sad and angry. Running inside, I went to the principal, Mr. Shannon, and asked him to get the marbles back. He called the boys over, questioned them about the incident, and looked into their faces. The older boys replied they were just "funning," and only teasing me because I won so much. I learned a lesson from that: "Take nothing for granted. What you think you have in the bag can get taken away quickly if you take your eyes off it." I didn't put it in those words back then, but I took the message to heart.

I found it difficult to "keep up with the Joneses" at school. Some of the older kids owned more clothes and had parents who gave them more money to spend. Some classmates made fun of me, the poor farm boy, because I didn't have much and never had a lot of money. After a while, I realized that I just had to ignore them, go to school, and work on the farm.

The teacher was strict about us reading, writing, and spelling. She would call on us to read sentences from the frayed readers, spell out certain words, and give the meanings of the words. If one child failed to wither under her questioning, she called on the next one in the row. The boys sat on one side of the room, while the girls sat on the other side. I'm sorry now that I didn't pay more attention in school. I really didn't focus on school and book learning. I was not a bad boy, but I did get into my share of trouble. Mr. Shannon constantly told me that I was a good kid. "You're not as bad as people say that you are," he said to me. "But I have to keep my eye on you anyway."

I had a master strategy, a clever plan to charm my teachers and distract them from looking at what I did not accomplish in school. Smiling sheepishly, I would present them with eggs and sweet potatoes and told them that my mother sent the gifts. If I hadn't done the homework, I would just grin and explain that I forgot to bring it. I would give them a long explanation and they would tell me to bring it later, which I never did. I hated homework. When the presents ceased to work, I picked colorful flowers from the yards of my neighbors and put together tasteful bouquets to set on their desks. Many of my teachers got so caught up in the flowers that they forgot all about my homework.

Going to school was an outlet, an escape from home and the farm, but sometimes I was very tired by the time I got to school, after getting up at five in the morning and doing my chores and walking three miles to class. I liked my school, my teachers, and friends and would have liked to spend more time with them. As I got older, I liked the girls, but the only time I could really talk to a girl was on Sunday, because after school I always had to hurry home and do the evening chores. I wonder now whether I would have married one of those girls if I had stayed.

Other than school, church was the occasion where boys and girls could sit together without their parents fussing. "Going to meeting" was the big event of the week because it brought us all together as a unified community. Whenever people who had gone away came back for a visit, they always came on a church day so they could see everybody and be seen. They could let everybody know they had succeeded in life, had "made it," and done well for themselves.

Church was where we could sing and laugh and worship as we pleased. Church was one of the only places where the signs of Jim Crow in public places, FOR COLORED and FOR WHITES, were not present and did not matter. Church was the place where kids could look nice—hair combed, faces washed, and clothes neat.

Traditionally, folks stayed at church all day on Sunday. When we came home Sunday night, we looked forward to eating some more good food, and we were still charged up from playing with our friends at church. That was the one time my father did not say anything about our excitement. He just let us play.

WHEN I WAS GROWING UP, life in Summerton hadn't changed much since the Civil War. The majority of the land there was owned by white people, who were large landowners renting or contracting out their fields to blacks; seven out of every ten people in the county were black and nearly every one of those lived on a farm. My father was a sharecropper, working 25 acres of his own land but plowing and planting crops on 175 rented acres of field owned by a white man. That was not uncommon around there.

Clarendon County, where we lived, was 600 square miles of farm and pasture, broken up by woodlands of gum trees, oaks, and pines. To the eye, it was flat, marshy land. They call it low country, but it is not as low as right along the scenic coast. If you know South Carolina first-hand, you know that a plain cuts across the state, dividing the rich coastal country from the sand hills.

Summerton, with the surrounding communities of St. Paul, Davis Station, Cross Roads, and Goat Island, was about sixty miles inland. The town was originally called "Summertown" when it was founded by white plantation owners who desired a kind of resort community where their wives and children could escape for a time from the harsh summer heat. Blacks worked as cooks, servants, nannies, and lawn men in the more affluent resorts. However, the land in Summerton was still fertile enough for black folk to grow good crops, depending on the amount of rain to nourish the plants. The trick, according to good farmers, was to get enough moisture to quench a plant's thirst but not enough to drown it. It was a delicate balance. Too dry was worse than too wet. The weather could be fickle sometimes and the farmers knew it.

"We need some rain in the worst way," my father would say, standing over the parched soil. "We don't want the plants to burn up."

A week later, my father would say that he wished the rain would stop so the crops could catch a breath from all the moisture. Whenever we prayed, it seemed, we prayed about the rain but the message to the Almighty switched back and forth between "Lord, please let it rain" and "Lord, please let this rain stop."

In early spring, when the rains started to wane, my father and other farmers plowed the earth and planted cotton, corn, oats, wheat, tomatoes, cucumbers, soybeans, watermelons, field peas, butter beans, sweet peas, and other vegetables. We raised sweet corn for eating while putting aside the other corn crop for feeding to the hogs and cows.

There were three ways to farm back in those days if you did not own the land—and few of the blacks owned land. First, if you could afford to rent, you paid eight dollars an acre, and then you farmed the land with your own fertilizer, mule, and equipment. Second, you could contract-farm, a slow process where you would get paid a dollar or two by the week for your labor. If you stayed there until harvesttime, you would get a bonus determined by the owner for the abundance of the crops. I did not know any families that took part in this contract process.

Or a farmer could sharecrop. This meant the white man owned everything, including the land, the fertilizer, the mules, and the equipment. Sometimes a farming family would be advanced food for the season: hog meat, two chickens, millet, cornmeal, and molasses. The cost of the food would be deducted from the profits at harvesttime. The black people provided the muscle and sweat, laboring in the sun, which burned in your chest as you cleared the stubborn weeds around your precious crops. Whatever way you farmed, using any of the three methods, you got a free house for your family. But unfortunately, despite the plentiful crops of the harvest, some farmers came up short and had to borrow money and food to tide them over until the next harvest season.

My father paid $320 a year to the McClarys for the use of his land. No one in the family knows where he got the money to get his start, but the deal was made with a handshake and a promise to do his best. He was a tireless worker, laboring long after others were panting from the heat and sore muscles, and he never complained. Farming was a daily responsibility. It was not an easy life.

Looking back, I realize that my father believed a man's character was molded by hard work, determination, and keeping your word. Like most southern black men, he trusted in the credo of Booker T. Washington, that a man could be lifted by the mastery of his trade, sweat, and perseverance. Maybe he was like so many farmers who had large families with lots of children, potential workers to take their place in the field. They hoped to harvest the crops with a profit so that they could overcome the huge debt put on them by white owners.

My father was very strict with us, and he never gave us gifts of any kind, except around Christmastime. This was when I got new overalls and a pair of shoes. Holidays were fun when everybody came together, laughing and playing. We also hung stockings over the fireplace and got candles and trinkets in them. My father was the best provider. Nobody went hungry. Some men escaped their families and responsibilities, going north, but he never did. His family was everything to him.

What did my father look like? I can still see him in my mind's eye so clearly. He had rough skin, straight black hair, and bushy eyebrows. Later in my life, I would come to think that he resembled President Richard Nixon with his profile and his notable eyebrows. I don't think my father was a man to fret, stew over past mistakes, or be sentimental. He liked his privacy, going off by himself. Occasionally, he would get together with his men friends at a café on a Saturday night, drinking and listening to the live music there. My mother did not object because she knew he worked hard during the week. We boys respected yet feared my father because he was a man of action and few words. He didn't talk much except to get a point across to us.

My brother Charlie was a prankster who was always into something and blaming it on me. I was a soft touch. I tried not to make a fuss at first, but my parents knew how Charlie was. At school, it took the teacher a long time to realize that it was Charlie who hid the pencils or made funny faces when her back was turned, not me.

Still, Charlie would lie with a straight face, and say innocently: "My brother Bertie did it." He could be very convincing when he tried. When I got older, I always thought Charlie could be a salesman or even a politician.

Charlie, whose nickname was Cherokee, was a handsome guy with straight hair just like my father's. As he got older, he had a beautiful gray streak going through his hair that the girls really liked. Most of my brothers were born with straight hair, but I had nappy hair. And you know with colored folk, hair was everything.

When Charlie graduated from school, he departed for New York City, seeking a better life there than he found in the segregated South. Although my father did not like his leaving the farm, he did not raise a ruckus. Charlie's actions inspired my brother John to dream of escaping Summerton.

Escaping, or "going up the road" as the locals put it, was a very common dream among blacks in our town in the 1930s and '40s. Plenty of blacks from the fields ran off to the northern cities of Chicago, Detroit, Washington, D.C., New York City, Philadelphia, and Baltimore. During this time, my older brother Robert had already joined the Marine Corps and another brother, John, was also on his own.

While I was still a little boy, my father decided he wanted to move across the road to another house for a little more space. He wanted to stretch out. The new house, constructed of brick, had a couple more rooms and a bigger barn. Folks thought the house was kind of "modern"-style for those days. Very fancy. Along with four bedrooms, the house contained a large kitchen with an enormous stove. We had no electricity back then, so we used kerosene lamps or candles, which my mother worried would hurt our eyes. Refrigeration meant buying huge blocks of ice from the icehouse in town to keep the food packed so that it remained cool and unspoiled.

Like many of the houses in town, our place had no indoor plumbing. We didn't even know what a kitchen sink was. For fresh water, there was a well with a hand pump and sometimes you got a workout just to get a decent amount in the bucket. The toilet was in an outhouse situated a good distance from the house. You wanted to put the outhouse as far away as possible and hope that when the wind blew hard it would not be blowing in your direction. At night, our family used a slop bucket in the house rather than going all the way to the outhouse.

There was no green, manicured lawn around our house, just a yard of weeds that my brothers and I cut with a scythe while my sisters kept it neat by sweeping. When the yard was clean, the sand on top was the color and consistency of beach sand. Summerton is only sixty miles from Myrtle Beach. Whereas the soil on the farm was a gray-brown color, when it was plowed it turned up the tinge of a red clay. When Martin Luther King, Jr. frequently referred to the red hills of Georgia, it reminded me of the brick color of the ground back home. I used to love to plow that soil with the blade and the ox because it made me feel like a big man. My father put me to work when I was ten years old. I was doing a man's work when I was belt-high: weeding, planting, and plowing. The grown-ups praised my father for rearing me right, to be a hard worker like him. Now, other kids my age did little chores around the house, sweeping or mopping, but they did not plow or run the heavy equipment.

I plowed barefoot in the fields, day in and day out, with my shoeless feet in the earth. That was a good feeling. I still like to walk around with no shoes on. We had to wash our dirty feet in a basin on the back porch before we went into the house. We only wore shoes in the winter, because it got too cold to do otherwise. There was a time when I was proud to be a farmer's son. Turning over that red soil gave me a good feeling, because I could look down the row I had just done and know that I had accomplished something. It was also wonderful to know my brothers thought I could earn my keep. After I finished a day's work, Robert would pat me on the back and say that I was doing a good job. That felt great.

Robert later told me, long after I left the farm, that my father thought I was one of his best workers. I knew that nobody had to stand over me to see if I did the job. I just did it. But my father never spoke a word about the quality of my work to me. There were no compliments from my father. In fact, he wouldn't say anything, but sometimes I would catch him sitting there, studying me like he would look at a clear sky for a dark cloud.

WHEN MARCH CAME, the frosts were over, and it was time to get ready for planting. I assisted in the planting and cultivation of the cotton, corn, hay, field peas, wheat, oats, and tobacco. We didn't do much tobacco, only about an acre. The month of May brought the start of hot weather, and the mosquitoes, gnats, and flies swarmed out of the marshes and swamps and into the cotton fields where we worked. Some people were so used to them that they could no longer feel them. However, with the overpowering heat, others became sick from staying out in the fields too long and getting bitten so much.

In Summerton, malaria, "the fever," was a serious topic of talk during that time. Everyone was afraid of it because it had a very high death rate. The fever was caused by a mosquito-borne disease that produced high temperatures, chills, and flulike symptoms. Government officials say almost 30,000 people died from malaria in the southeastern states in the 1940s. Federal programs distributed fresh bed-nets, insecticides, and antimalaria drugs, and later quinine would be introduced in several coastal areas. Still, there were special roots and herbs used to combat the fever among local blacks and to make them well. The elders, at the first sign of the fever, would offer the ailing person feverfew for reducing the fever, white willow to heal inflamed organs and relieve night sweats, and burdock to purify the blood. In a few days, health would be restored.

"Cover yourself, boy, before you go into the field, because I don't want you to get the fever," Daddy told me. He wanted me to take every precaution against the disease. Since I covered myself with long pants and long-sleeved shirts in the field, I never got the fever, although I got bitten several times. I didn't know anyone personally who died from malaria, but word traveled to us that a number of people had perished from the disease.

We kids swam in the creek and often came home hot all over with a fever from the bugs. Whenever this happened to me or any of my siblings, my mother took a special flower, put it in a towel with alcohol and tied it around our heads. How funny we must have looked. I have no idea what the flower was but some say it was lavender. Unbelievable as it may seem, the home remedy always brought the fever down.

September was a happy time, because that was when the cotton was ready to pick, thus that was when everybody had money. I helped to bale the cotton. I was always thinking ahead. I remember putting a little water on the cotton to make it heavier so it would weigh as much as possible. Truthfully, I never felt the least bit guilty, because we all knew the cotton buyers fixed their scales so they could pay less than the crop was worth. They shortchanged us. When it was the buying season, the cotton gin stayed open all night for people transporting raw cotton for sale. There was grueling work to be done at harvesttime.

Once you gathered the cotton, you started with the stack cutter, a two-wheeled, sharp-bladed device pulled by two mules, which had a seat on which you could ride. Somehow, when I was eleven, I had an accident and got thrown off the cutter.

"What have you done, child?" my mother asked me, cradling my head.

"I fell off the cutter and it ran over my legs," I replied, trying not to look at my slashed limbs. I was determined to be brave, like a grown-up.

A few of the men carried me home, with my mother at my side and a blood-soaked blanket tossed over my legs. I refused to let my siblings see me cry. They placed me down on the bed and uncovered my legs to see the extent of my injuries. Today, of course, I would have been rushed to a hospital, received an antibiotic and stitches as treatment, but there wasn't any emergency room back then in Clarendon County for blacks. My mother knew what to do, wrapping some spiderwebs around my mangled legs to stop the bleeding. I was laid up for a long time, knowing full well that if my legs got infected I might lose them, but luckily no gangrene set into them.

SEVERAL MEMBERS OF MY FAMILY were located nearby in the tight-knit community. In fact, my grandmother's house was very close and one of my aunt's clan lived a few miles away. The landscape in the summer was lush, green, full of fruit trees and flowers. Down the way a piece was the Hemmingway farm, where I worked sometimes for spare change by picking boll weevils from the cotton plants in the field. The Hemmingways were white and owned over a thousand acres, like the McClarys, our landlords and owners of the cotton gin where we took our crop. John, my oldest brother, worked for the McClarys at their sawmill and other places. He was allowed to have a job of his own, so he would have his own money and not be totally dependent on working on our farm.

The boll weevils, which infested the cotton plants, could ruin a crop. I filled up a pint-sized can with the bugs in about a half a day for less than a quarter per can, supervised by the Hemmingway's son, Bubba, who made sure that the bottom of the can was not just stuffed with green leaves.

Bubba was about my age, and since we were neighbors we had played together since we were little kids. We loved to play marbles to-

gether. I beat him most of the time. Sometimes I allowed him to win because he was so bad at the game. In fact, he was terrible at sports—all
sports. When he played ball, kicking it back and forth in our made-up
games, I let him hit it over the line for a point every so often, just to
make the game more interesting. I was never athletic, but I was a champ
in comparison to Bubba Hemmingway.

Bubba and I sat around and talked a lot about coming to each
other's house to spend the night, having a sleepover of sorts. Neither of
us ever mentioned it to our parents. It was just something we discussed,
but it was not going to come true. Bubba was usually the one to bring it
up, I think, because he was curious about how we lived. We always
knew how white people lived because we worked in their homes, but
they never got into ours. We remained a mystery to them. When white
people sometimes came by our homes, we met them at the door,
whether they stopped to drop off clothes for my mother to wash or to
get something from the garden. We did not let them enter.

Bubba's father, Mr. Hemmingway, was a rough-looking man,
around six-foot-four, weighing about two-hundred pounds. I never
really saw his wife or his daughters, since they always put the food out
for us when they fed us some lunch during our workday in the fields.
They made sure that we were a distance from the house and went hur-
riedly back through the door to "safety." The lunch wasn't anything
much: syrup and biscuits or cornbread, sometimes a baloney or peanut-
butter sandwich, and always a glass of milk.

For the main shopping in Summerton, we stopped at the Hemmingway's small store, which was a short foot from their house. If you
wanted to get something from there, such as sardines or candy or cookies, you could buy them, but you wouldn't receive any money after
working all day. That was the arrangement. Even worse, depending on
what you got, you sometimes owed the Hemmingways and had to come
back the following day to work it off.

The McClarys owned a bigger store that also sold clothes, along
with tractors and all the latest farm equipment. Mr. McClary was a busi-
nessman, a wheeler-dealer whom I never saw, since he was always in his
office. He employed only white workers at the store, and most black

folks had no reason to go in his place, because they could not afford his farm equipment.

We all preferred the general store in town, which was owned by Mr. McDougal, who would let us trade goods for goods, unlike the other store owners, who liked to work it out of you. Old man McDougal was a short, fat man, who looked as though he'd eaten plenty of food the black folks brought. He was happy all of the time, laughing and joking with everybody, even the black kids who came in with the stuff to sell.

McDougal's store was one of my major sources for pocket change and movie money. I sold them eggs at the general store and put the money in my pocket. It was the first money I made without my father's permission. You might even call it stealing but it was not. We had so many chickens laying so many eggs that we children would take a few occasionally and sell them to McDougal. And my father never missed them. If he had noticed, we would have stopped doing it.

I got so brave I started taking chickens into McDougal's store, too. He paid more for a chicken than for a dozen eggs, depending on how much the chicken weighed. A plump bird was the best, for a few dollars more. McDougal asked us if my father sent the chicken and eggs to sell, checking to see if everything was legal. I nodded my head and said yes. He probably suspected I was not being truthful, but he took the stuff anyway.

Getting more efficient at my trade, I took the eggs or chickens either during the night or early in the morning when my father was asleep. We children had to do the chores so we were up anyway. I hid the chickens down by a ditch bank a short distance from the house. To make sure that the birds didn't make a fuss, I tied up the hens' legs to a tree, knowing a hen won't make a noise when she's bound with a string.

All them chickens we have out here, Daddy won't miss one, I kept thinking to myself. I knew I had to keep my father from finding out or he'd tan my hide.

When I made the exchange of the chicken, old man McDougal looked me in the face, examining me for any sign of larceny. "Boy, are you sure your father sent this bird in?" he questioned me. "I don't want to get into any trouble with him."

"Yes sir, sure did," I replied with a straight face.

I hated the next question from him. "Has this chicken been in the clean house?"

I shook my head, saying no. A clean house was built out of chicken wire, and it was where a farmer would isolate a chicken for a week and feed it just corn and water before it was killed. You weren't supposed to take a chicken from the yard to slaughter without putting it in the clean house first, because a bird running around would eat anything on the ground and was not considered "clean." When it was placed in the clean house, you controlled what the chicken ate, and ensured the quality of health of the bird. In those days, a chicken was a luxury item, and we didn't eat it as we do now. Fried chicken, for example, was a special, delicious treat, which we got once in a blue moon.

Everything we needed was at McDougal's: food, clothes, medicine, and dry goods. It was our equivalent of Wal-Mart, one-stop shopping. One of the attractions of McDougal's store was a place in the back where he carried a variety of herbs and roots. The elders believed in the potency and magic of these natural remedies, like peppermint for the digestive system, sarsaparilla for purifying the blood, and fenugreek for diabetes or "sugar." Some swore by the power of tree moss, which was supposed to lower high blood pressure if you placed it in your shoes.

At McDougal's place, they had witch-doctor stuff, too, and things for hoodoo spells. They had big, dark bottles of the herbs and roots on countless shelves and small boxes of charms underneath the counter. Sometimes I would peek in there and see the people asking for the ingredients of the spells: nettles for removing curses and hexes, motherwort to keep one's family safe, life everlasting tea for prolonging life, king of the woods for control over a woman, licorice to keep lovers faithful, cinnamon for success in money matters, adder's-tongue to stop gossip and slander, and juniper berries and trumpet weed to revive a man's nature. I never believed in such hoodoo spells but many of the old people did.

Several people who knew about herbs were healers, too. They

knew just what flower or plant to get from the fields to steep as a tea, or stir into your food or drink. They taught our mothers what to use for disease and low spirits. Today we have TV commercials about drugs that can solve our sexual problems, yet Mr. McDougal could have sold you something for that, too! We were very dependent in those times on the local healers' knowledge, because we lived in a black county without an accredited black doctor.

Occasionally, Summerton would get a glimpse of the life outside of our small hamlet when several rich plantation owners came to spend the summers there, giving us a peep at their lavish lifestyle. Wearing custom-made white suits and white summer dresses, they brought the maids, chauffeurs, and yard men with them, so they could live in high style. The chauffeurs, with their neat uniforms and hats, came behind the McDougal store to wash their cars and talk to their fellow drivers. Kids like me gathered to watch and hung on their every word. Most of the drivers said they had a great life, were well compensated, and had a sense of freedom unknown to those living on the farm.

"You don't have to work the fields?" I asked them.

"We're chauffeurs," they explained proudly, leaning against their long, shiny cars. "Our job is to take care of the cars and drive them around."

What a good life, I thought to myself, conjuring up all of the drudgery of working on a farm. *Dressing up in a shirt and tie and nice suit and driving all day long! No mud. No gathering crops or feeding the pigs. That is for me, the good life.*

That thought of freedom continued to dog me. My favorite holiday when I was a kid was the Fourth of July. It was the only summer holiday permitted for fun and frolic by black folks, which was sanctioned by the white landlords. They gave us that day off. We did not waste it. Our big-city relatives came home from places like Washington, D.C., New York, Baltimore, Philadelphia, and Florida, driving beautiful, fast cars and looking like a million dollars in their best clothes. Their families were very glad to see them, especially since most of the men mailed large cash advances in letters to pave their way. The fathers and mothers bragged about how well their sons were doing in the North. Everything was to impress the families they had left behind. However, their sons went into steep debt to get their pricey cars and clothes, so they could change their suits twice a day and ride their kinfolk around through town after town.

Like royalty, their sons entered the Liberty Hill African Methodist Episcopal Church, the biggest church in town, in a group with still another wardrobe change, tugging on their lapels, walking calmly as a celebrity would do. They stood up for recognition by the congregation. The ladies always sat on one side of the church, dressed in white, and the men on the other side, dressed in dark suits. After service was over, Reverend Richburg shook their hand, noted their prosperity, and wished them well. Then the men went on a tour from house to house, getting pats on the backs and high praise. You may think the letters "R&B" stood for "rhythm and blues," but in those days to the black people from Summerton who had "gone up the road" it was short for "renting and borrowing." They rented fancy cars to drive to their old community and borrowed fine clothes in order to look as affluent as possible. Everyone returned in high style, even if it was a style that just lasted a weekend.

No other holiday in South Carolina was celebrated like Independence Day, or "Homecoming" as the folks called it. Even Thanksgiving and Christmas were low-key efforts when compared to the Fourth of July. Preparations for the arrival of relatives began right after the crops were planted. This was called the "lay-by" time, during which I think we were waiting for the crops to grow.

It was a busy time. The ladies shelled pecans, gathered peaches, picked watermelons, and prepared the cakes and pies for their friends and loved ones. My father and the other men joined in to dig the barbecue pit for the roasted pig, which was the main course of the meal. The men took turns perfecting the sauce used to spice the grilled pork flesh. It was a joyous time. The whole cooking process for the barbecue took two or three days.

I followed our visitors, the big-city relatives, around when they arrived on the holiday. They could see by my face that I was very impressed when they unpacked their big suitcases. "Is this your suit? Are all these clothes yours?"

"Yeah, when you go up the road, you make a lot of money and you can buy all this stuff," they told me, laying out their clothes. "You got nobody telling you what to do with your money and how many suits to buy." It wasn't until later that I found out most of these suits did not belong to them. All of the finely dressed visitors were bragging victims of R&B.

But their new cars held the utmost fascination for me. My eyes got big looking at all the cars, the sedans with the luxurious interiors, which nobody in my town owned. Outside of our house, my relatives babied the cars parked there, shining the hood, sides, and chrome bumpers, and wiping down the tires. They allowed me to sit in the driver's seat and pretend I was driving. When my cousins came out, I didn't have to walk anywhere. Every family had relatives visiting who were driving shiny cars and wearing fancy clothes. It was like a competition. One family tried to outdo the others and everyone went to other people's houses to show off. There was plenty of competition over the food offerings on the Fourth, too. If one family lacked a certain dish, it could be found in another home. The families were very generous, inviting people into their homes, offering them their warm hospitality.

"Come on in, get a plate," the neighbors said, smiling. "Have some food. Get off your feet and sit a spell."

When the men gathered around under the big oak tree and began telling stories about their life in the big city, everything they owned, the great jobs they had, and how much better life was "up the road" in the northern cities, I was a sponge. I listened intently to every word. It was a custom to demonstrate your wealth and success by giving the kinfolks "a big piece of change," so when the cousins brought the tribute of money to my parents, they were very grateful. I don't know exactly how much they gave Mama, but she was pretty happy getting it. I guess she was very pleased since this would be her own personal money and could be spent on what she desired. Even on those occasions when my father was broke, my mother would tell him she didn't have any money, so she could hang on to what she had saved.

One of the relatives most impressive to me was my cousin Willie, who had left the farm, journeyed to Washington, D.C., and made his fortune there. Everybody eagerly waited for him to arrive in Summerton. His arrival was the most anticipated among my relatives. He drove back home in a big, fancy automobile and owned an extensive wardrobe; he changed outfits at least twice a day while visiting the South.

When I was twelve, I took Willie aside before he left to go back. "Willie, do they have farms up North?" I asked him. I knew he would give me a honest answer.

"No," he answered as he wiped away a smudge on his new black patent leather shoe.

"Really?" I was bewildered because I thought everything was like our town.

He laughed and patted me on my shoulder. "Man, you'll never see a farm again once you get to D.C. The farther north you go, the farther you'll be from farming. All you'll see is lights, paved streets, and all kinds of cars. Folks walk around busy, just hustle-and-bustle, going to work. The city is so different from around here."

"What about horses and mules?"

Again he grinned, teasing me about how innocent I was. "No . . . no . . . no, you don't see no mules, and the only horses you're gonna see are the ones they run on a track for a race to bet on. And the only chickens and pigs you see is on the dinner table."

That sounded like heaven to me, because I had been working on a farm from age six and the chore I hated most was "slopping the hogs." I looked forward to someday living in a place where I never had to do that again. The return of the men reinforced that dream in me. Honestly, I didn't like the farm that much. Until I heard the stories from up North, there was nothing to compare with farm life, especially against the dream of the promised land "up the road." I thought the whole world lived like my family. It was hard, but we got along as long as we knew "our place" and to say "yessuh" and "nosuh." We knew that Jim Crow meant letting the white man go first in line all the time. Our parents told us to do that so we would not get in trouble. As a farm boy at heart, I still say "sir" to everyone, black and white.

Other than the big-city relatives and the chauffeurs, my older brother Robert was my hero. I was ten years old when he left the farm, packed up, and joined the Marines. I knew that my brother had been drafted into the Marines, but I had no idea at that time that he was in a war or even that the United States was at war. I did not know what a war was. We never listened to the radio because we didn't have any electricity or a battery-powered radio. We didn't even have a newspaper in town.

"No matter what the color of the person, if you treat people right, they will treat you right," Robert told me when I was very young. I never forgot that.

On the Fourth of July, 1944, Robert, the new Marine, came home on a military furlough, ramrod straight as a fresh recruit. I was awed by how my favorite brother looked in that uniform, the smart green uniform with the shirt neatly pressed and the sharp, creased pants. I was so proud of Robert. He was the same old Robert, calm and collected, just more so. My parents were proud of him as well. No matter how good the up-North relatives looked in those rented suits, Robert looked better than them all, wearing his Marine uniform.

Other than the northern relatives and Robert telling me a story, the only stories I got was when I started going to the movies in town. The theater owners featured newsreels, three-to-five minutes of films with bits of travel and historic events, playing with the movies, but I never thought of the newsreels as "real" or truth. For me, the newsreels were just part and parcel of the fantasy and magic of the movies. Besides, black people did not appear in the newsreels. If a black person appeared in a movie, it was in a small role. But we were glad to see them up there, no matter what they were doing. In the forties, all they showed in the newsreels was white people running around with guns shooting at other white people in war, which was pretty much the same thing they showed in the regular movies.

The thing I understood was the stories where attractive white men and women starred in comedies, wars, romances, musicals, and westerns with images of a world that I had never seen. I only imagined this kind of life. To an isolated farm boy, the world was divided into black and white, and white faces were white faces, whether they came from the United States, Germany, or even Japan. Although I saw war in the newsreels, World War II and its widespread violence did not make it into my consciousness. I believe black people in Summerton at that time did not have the energy to worry about anything other than their own survival. What was happening overseas never came up in conversation.

Even though I did not really understand the newsreels, going to the movies was something I craved. I was fascinated by the exploits of Roy Rogers, John Wayne, Clark Gable, James Cagney, Edward G. Robinson, and Spencer Tracy. The women were equally appealing to me: Loretta Young, Rita Hayworth, Betty Grable, Maureen O'Hara, Myrna Loy, and Rosalind Russell. Unfortunately, my moviegoing was expensive.

If I asked my father for "movie money," he frowned and looked out at the fields. "Go ask your mother," he said on more than one occasion.

"I already did," I answered. "She said to ask you."

"Well then, I reckon you ain't going," he said firmly. "We ain't got no money for such foolishness."

We didn't have enough to spare, but my determination to go to the movies was driving me. Either I would earn the money from others or get it some other way. I loved going to the movies. Under Jim Crow, the movie house had a WHITE ONLY sign for one door and a COLORED sign for the other door. The whites sat together in the best seats on the first floor, and the blacks were seated on the floor above, which someone derisively called "The Buzzard's Roast," but we still had fun. When you have birds perched in a tree, you don't want to be standing underneath, if you know what I mean. After a while, the whites remedied this situation by making everyone sit on the first floor, but still segregated into black and white sections.

I was annoyed that my father refused to give me the little amount of movie money I requested. The movie fare was only fifteen cents. He kept shoeboxes with each of our names on them in an old wooden chest into which he frequently put money. The more work I did in the field, the more money he placed into the box. Mr. McClary, the landowner of our field, required my father to keep a close record of the total money earned by the children, and my father kept his accounts in order by using the shoeboxes.

"This is your box, boy," my father said to me.

Before the summer of 1944, a refusal from my father did not seem so hard to take, but as I entered into my teens that year, I became a different boy. Then there was the shining vision of Robert, my favorite brother, with his neat uniform in the military. The additional allure of the chauffeurs and the big-city relatives with their new cars and fine clothes began to alter my awareness—I could do better than this small world in Summerton. The make-believe world of the movies fed me enough reasons to leave the dreariness of farm life, and after all, my parents let Robert go into the service. But would they let me go north? What would my father say?

When school started up again, I was restless, not as happy as I had been in previous years. Even my old teacher, Mrs. Blackwell, noticed I was not my "jolly self at the opening of school" after the summer. She told me years later when I came back for a visit that she remembered clearly that I was sad and unproductive during my last days in her class. I remembered them that way, too.

Often I daydreamed about how I would make my escape, but then I would go over the good times I'd had in Summerton. That saddened me. The crazy jokes and teasing at the barbershop on Saturday, listening to the music coming out of the windows at the cafés, and eating crispy fried fish all tugged at my heartstrings. Also, I loved sweets. I would miss my mother's tasty coconut pie, tangy cherry pie, and even the delicious pineapple pie. As I sprawled in the tall grass, I recalled the homemade ice cream we made with a crank bucket turned by hand, using salt to melt the ice from the icehouse. Everybody would take turns churning the ice cream. We got fresh peaches off the trees and picked strawberries, and then made fresh peach or strawberry ice cream. Oh, what flavor!

I loved my mother's cooking. We would crack pecans from the previous year's crop, and she would mix it up to make butter pecan ice cream. Where could I get a chunk of pound cake with rich butter, sugar, and all of the spices? My mother's specialty was a flavorful apple jelly cake, and though I was very small when Bertha, my older sister, got married, I still remember the huge cake my mother baked for the occasion, piled up five layers high, with that sweet apple jelly between the layers. Where would I get cooking like this in the North?

That October, I took a couple of chickens to Mr. McDougal's store to exchange for something my mother needed in the kitchen. I grabbed the chickens, stuffed them into my pants-legs and walked into the store.

When I got there late that Saturday afternoon, it looked like the Fourth of July all over again. There was energy and excitement in the air as I noticed a large crowd of very important-looking people gathered in front of the store.

Surrounded by placards reading "Maybank for U.S. Senate," a tall, burly-looking white man was shaking hands with the men, hugging the old folk, and kissing babies. Some of his aides were passing out campaign buttons to anybody who walked past. The street in front of McDougal's store was packed with large, long sedans, parked to carry the big campaign entourage. All the cars had black chauffeurs, who had gathered in a group in back of the store. The drivers, dressed in fine-looking uniforms, seemed to be having a good time eating and exchanging jokes and stories while they waited for the political rally to finish up.

I walked over to listen to what the politician was saying. After a while, I returned to ask the drivers questions about what they did, and they told me how much they liked their jobs. It must have been a great life driving those big cars around in South Carolina and "up the road" in Washington, D.C. How I envied them.

When the politician completed his speech, he started to walk through the crowd. I could finally see him up close. He was dressed in a nice suit and tie, and seemed very friendly and sincere. One of the chauffeurs told me this man's name was Senator Burnet Maybank, and he was a very popular fellow with a lot of power.

"If you ever get up to Washington, D.C.," Senator Maybank shouted out to the crowd, which gave out a loud roar in response, "drop by and see me."

As the young senator was about to enter his car, I went right up to him. He turned toward me with a warm smile. "If I come to Washington, can I come by and see you, too?" I asked him.

The senator leaned over and replied graciously, "Certainly, my boy." Then he got into his fancy car. I watched the entire line of shiny automobiles drive off up the road.

Every thought in my mind at that time was about "going up the road" and doing something other than farming. Somehow I was not afraid. I thought about it all the time: when I walked to school, when I was plowing, when I was feeding the animals. It was my obsession. If I left Summerton, I knew I was not going to fail as long as there was a way to make a nickel. I wasn't going to come back with my tail between my legs like so many of the local boys. I was honest and could make a decent living. I was a hard worker and I was going to succeed.

Everyone in the black community seemed to want to go "up the road" some time in the future. My older brother John had already run away once to Florida, leaving town with some relatives. However, my father went searching for him and brought him back. I carefully planned my exit: I wanted to leave on a train, and I wanted to go north, because I did not think my father would be able to find me if I lost my-self in a big city there.

To tell the truth, my running away was not really an impulsive act. Even before coming in contact with the chauffeurs or Senator Maybank or the cozy life of Willie in Washington, I dreamed of leaving the farm someday. For as long as I can remember, the escape plan was there, big as life, in the back of my mind. I always kept it closely guarded. I wanted to seize control of my life before anything other than me shaped it. I even took precautions about my departure, being very careful that I not dream about it so my brothers, who slept in the same bed with me, would not hear me talk about my plan in my sleep.

The only person I ever told about my plan was Rufus, my little brother, but I never let him know about my timetable. Still, he knew enough to tattle to my father—after I left. He could have told my parents on the morning following my departure, but he did not. I owe Rufus a lot for that. I knew that my leaving the farm would be seen as an act of defiance against my father and his authority.

That night, when I got home from school, my father made us work extra fast, rushing to beat the darkness of the night. Stressed about get-ting to market on time, he pressed us to get the cotton up into the wagon so we could haul it to the cotton gin in the morning. We finally finished the evening chores, muscles aching and sweating heavily, and ate dinner. I stood, looking at the cotton and the wagon. I was bone-tired.

I couldn't take this anymore. No more farm work. I don't know why but I said to myself, "This is it."

My father inspected the wagon to make sure that we had done a good job. He walked around it to check that the load was evenly distributed. Everyone was pretty tired, so I knew we were going to bed soon.

Quietly, I spotted an empty flour sack in a corner of the kitchen. I took the sack into the bedroom. I did not have many clothes, but I owned one suit that my mother had bought at a flea market. Putting the suit in the sack, I laid my overalls and some underwear and socks in it before tucking it in a set of dresser drawers. When everyone fell asleep and everything got quiet, I tiptoed through the dark rooms of the house. I opened the wooden chest and removed the money in the shoe box. Probably it was a lot less than fifty dollars, but I considered it then to be a small fortune. Creeping, I took my sack and eased out the front door and into the cotton field.

As I changed my clothes, I put on my suit and best shoes among the plucked cotton plants and the rows of dark soil. I felt a pang of sadness, leaving my family behind, but it quickly passed as I walked into the Summerton bus station. I was determined to stick with my plan. My goal was to take a bus to the Sumter train station, where I would board a train headed for the "promised land." I would not come back until I could consider myself a success.

⊷≫ TWO ≪⊶

A Boy Goes to Washington

I DON'T KNOW WHY IT WAS SO IMPORTANT FOR ME TO JOURNEY TO Washington after I saw Senator Maybank, but I think it was the greatest thing I did in my life, a bold move that most kids my age were afraid to make. For some reason, I felt confident that night when I bought my bus ticket. Maybe it was because I did not know the real dangers of the outside world away from Summerton. Probably if I had understood everything that could have happened to me, I would have stayed within the warm cocoon of my father's house.

On buses in those days, colored folks were only permitted in a separate section, usually in the back of the vehicle. If the bus was crowded, you had to give a white person your seat. I was relieved that there were enough seats that night for the whites, so the bus driver did not have to put me off the bus. I found a seat way in the back so no one would notice me. Occasionally, someone would look at me curiously, probably wondering why this young boy was traveling alone, but nobody bothered me. I kept looking out the window for the bridge over the railroad track because I knew that landmark was near the train station. I smiled politely, nodded graciously, and said hello to the other colored people, but I did not talk. I was eager to not miss my stop.

Nobody asked me how old I was or why I was traveling by myself so late at night. We traveled twenty miles or more, making about fifteen stops before finally reaching the station near the bridge. It was the biggest bridge I was ever to cross, although I did not know it then. In my young mind, it became a symbol of my journey—no turning back, and full speed ahead. In a short time, I looked up and all the passengers exited the bus.

I had never ridden the train so I did not know how to proceed.

"This man has a car, and he is taking people to the train station," some man said. "There's room for one more."

I quickly slid into the car before anyone could notice. As a young boy, I finally discovered that I could be fairly invisible to grown-ups and I took advantage of that newly acquired skill. It was a very short car trip, costing me fifty cents. But then at the station, I felt lost again, as all I saw was a sign proclaiming "white only." White folk rushed all around me, going every which way, and I looked totally confused. I stood there for a while until a white man noticed me.

"If you want to get the train, you have to go around there," the man said gruffly. He pointed in a general direction off to the left, around a corner where a group of black people were walking.

I must have looked as though I needed help. Imagine me with a Sunday suit, new shoes, and a slightly frayed flour sack under one arm. A black man glanced at me, shook his head, and showed me to the proper entrance. Shyly, I asked him how to get the train and he took me to the ticket clerk.

"This boy here wants to go to Washington, D.C.," he said to the clerk.

"That train is gone," the clerk said, frowning.

I asked when I could get the next one. Both the man and the clerk looked at their watches, glanced at the schedule board of arrivals and departures and took me aside. I was bewildered.

The clerk nodded and smiled at me. "The next train won't be until tomorrow morning. You can get that one then."

I did not know what to do. A young boy with so many questions in his head.

"Well, you can't stay here, because the colored station closes at ten o'clock," the clerk said, placing his pale hand on my shoulder.

Close to our group, a colored man, who was in charge of cleaning the station, overheard us and volunteered that he lived in a rooming house nearby. He added that he could talk to the lady there and see if she would put me up for the night. I couldn't believe my luck. When the clerk went back to his chores, I followed the cleaning man and assisted him in sweeping and mopping the floor. I emptied the trash baskets.

"You're a great help, boy," the cleaning man said, smiling over his shoulder as I dumped the garbage into a bin with wheels on it. The place smelled of the sharp tang of cleaning liquid, a mixture of lemon and strong bleach.

I grinned at his praise. My father had never given me such praise, even though I worked for him until my hands were full of blisters.

"What's your name?" the man asked

"Bertie, Bertie Bowman." My eyes were lowered to what I was doing.

Nobody had ever talked to me like this. "Well, you remember this," the man said firmly. "The important thing about a colored boy is that he can never forget himself. He can never let down his guard. The only thing he can control is his mind and his body, so he can never forget his place. Be responsible. Be mannerly. I've been up North and white folks are not like the ones you gonna find here. Some of them can be kind and caring by anybody's standards, but still be careful who you trust."

I nodded, absorbing what the man said. "Yessuh."

"And don't be a chatterbox, Bertie," the man added, motioning toward the white clerk. "Don't talk too much. Don't give up too much of your business. Most colored people who work around white folk can talk a lot about nothing. Cultivate that talent. Be good at it. You can have a personal opinion but don't give it."

I collected the brooms and pails full of dirty water. "Yessuh."

After we finished, I tagged along to where he lived, a small building with many rooms and people. It was quiet in the evening air. I wasn't scared, maybe because he had talked to me while we worked. It was not like it is today where a young boy must be on his guard, for anything could happen to him. I trusted the man. I put a few dollars in my pocket and stashed most of my money from the shoe box by pinning the dollar bills to my undershirt on my chest, the way I had seen the ladies do. I secured the money further with a belt around my waist to keep anything from falling out of my shirt.

I kept that money with me as carefully as those chickens I used to stuff in my overalls. Those chickens, although they put up a fight, did not get out and neither did my money. The cleaning man introduced me to the rooming-house lady, and her piercing eyes looked down suspiciously on my face, but her voice seemed very kind.

"So whose boy are you?" she asked.

I remained mute, not wanting to lie. I didn't want to slip up and be sent back before I could get to my destination.

"Cat got his tongue," the lady said, laughing. "Well, we will get you straight."

"He's shy," the cleaning man chuckled. "Doesn't say much."

After saying it was all right if I spent the night, she gave me a nice clean bed, and the next thing I knew somebody was pulling on my shoulder, saying it was time to get up. I didn't resist. The lady told me to wash up, offering me a pitcher, a basin of warm water, a big bar of homemade soap, and a towel. I washed up, cleaned the basin and put it back, spick-and-span. While I made up the bed, I smelled some good bacon frying in the kitchen. The landlady cooked a fine breakfast for the rooming house. She served grits and gravy, bacon, ham, eggs, fried apples, biscuits, and good strawberry jam, along with a big glass of milk. I love breakfast. It is my favorite meal, and I was happy that morning.

AROUND SIX THAT MORNING, the cleaning man told me that we must get over to the train station, the time was getting close for the caboose going north, and I couldn't be late. I thanked the lady for her kindness and asked her how much I owed. She grabbed my hand and replied I didn't owe her anything. Grateful, I tried to give her the money, the $2.50 stashed in my pocket, but nothing could touch her charity.

"No, son, you keep that," she said warmly. "You're going to Washington, the big city, and you may need it. In fact, I know you are going to need it to survive there."

As we departed, the lady called us back and gave each of us a bag packed with lunch. I was surprised that she gave me one, too. I hugged her and thanked her again. I know I was smiling all the way to the train.

If what is in this bag is as good as that breakfast was, I got some good eating going up the road, I thought. The lady reminded me of my mother's caring ways.

When we got to the station, the cleaning man helped me get my ticket for the train to Washington. I wished I could remember all those people's names who assisted me during that first trip. Many times, I have thought back at how honest, kind, and giving they were. Nobody really questioned me. To be honest, I don't know why these people helped me, but they did. I left home with almost nothing to go on my trip north but so many people reached out to me offering help and guidance. I would not advise any young person to do this today. Running away these days could have serious consequences, for this is a hard world. The elders back home always said of my journey that the angels were looking over me, and maybe this faith was what got me through.

Just think, I gave the fellow my ticket money, and he could have cheated me easily. I was a young country hick. I was so very trusting. Years later, when I went back home for the first time, I looked for these people so I could express my deep appreciation, my utmost gratitude, but I found the train station closed and the rooming house torn down.

Like a true friend, the cleaning man waited with me until the train came in, and then he took me to see one of the train's porters. I believed he was sorry to see me go.

"This is Bertie, and he is going to Washington, D.C.," the cleaning man said, pushing me gently in front of the porter. "He's a good boy. He helped me clean the station last night. Help him if you can."

The porter was an older man with gray hair and strong hands. He looked me over with friendly eyes. "Come with me," he said. "Take your stuff and put it under the seat. I want you to sit right here. You are in for a long day's ride."

Now, I was officially on my way, up the road, to the North. My heart thudded in my chest as I shook hands with the cleaning man for the final time. I would be grateful to him for the rest of my life. I sat down and looked out the window as the train pulled away. It was a new day. The sun's rays glinted off the buildings around the station as it rose above the trees.

BERTIE BOWMAN, you are only thirteen years old and here you are, on your way to the big city, I thought, feeling the seat under me. I watched the scenery from the windows, the flat landscape, and the farmers walking around in their fields in the distance.

My mind was closed to all things past. I was not going to look back on my farm days, hog slopping, or the long hours of toil. I didn't give a thought to things back at home. That train rolled on all day long, to the song of the metal against the tracks, the blur of the towns and villages moving past my eyes. I wasn't going to get to Washington until around eight o'clock that night, and I told the porter that I would be glad to work if he needed anyone to help him.

"We'll see," the porter said, very aware of the white conductor, who could make trouble for him if he wanted. "There's always something to do around here. But be careful of the conductor. He's in charge of the porters and attendants."

The conductor walked back and forth through the aisle, checking on the porters and attendants, all colored, making sure that everything was up to standard. I watched the porter, who kept out of his way but did his work. His job was to help with the bags, to meet the requests of the riders, and put out the steps when the train stopped. All the attendants worked in the kitchen, cooking meals and serving the commuters. I learned much on that train. Everything was so new and different in this environment outside of Summerton. It was my first experience in a much bigger world. For example, the train featured a flush toilet and I was only familiar with outhouses in my rural town.

As soon as the train made its first stop, I learned how to put down the steps, gracefully without much fanfare, and then I watched the porter assist the white ladies in all their finery off to the platform. We loaded their baggage onto carts. The colored passengers traveled in separate cars from the white people, cramped from inferior passage, and did not get the porters' assistance. They got off the best way they could. According to the rules, the colored riders could not put their bags on a cart; they had to carry them.

Later, after I had eaten my lunch of ham and bacon sandwiched between biscuits, I helped out in the kitchen cleaning off the tables, and they rewarded me by giving me a free dinner. I took the dinner back to my seat in the segregated car where all the colored passengers ate food that they had brought with them. In that time, we could not go on the train without taking along our own food and drink, because we could not buy any in the dining car. That was only for white people.

The train trip and helping those guys out were very positive experiences, ones that convinced me that I'd made the right decision. I could survive away from home. I knew I could survive in the big city. If I could help those men do their work, after all, I could certainly hold down a job when I got to the city. Unlike some of the young guys, I was not too serious about myself. I could get along with anybody. The porter and the attendant seemed to like me, kidding me constantly, joking that I acted as though I was just hired on.

"Are you trying to take over our jobs?" they asked me. As it turned out, it wasn't just a joke, because later, when the train got close to Washington, they asked if I would really like a job on the train. They also said the white conductor said he would hire me because of the excellent work I had done that day.

But I had a mission. One mission alone: to be a success in the city. I told them no. The main reason I did not take that job was that it interfered with the game plan I'd had in my head for so long. I was going to go to the city, where I could get a job wearing a uniform, wearing a hat, and driving a shiny car. Who wanted to go back down South? I knew I would like it here, with its opportunities. I knew I could do a lot of growing up here and mature into quite a man. Also, the porter informed me a lot about his work schedule, and how he would work without any time off all the way from the South to New York City and back again. It sounded almost as exhausting as farm work.

When the train pulled into Washington, I had never seen so many lights. It was like the world was on fire. As I gathered my stuff, the porter asked me again if I wanted the train job.

"No," I said. "I am finally in the city. This is what I have been waiting for all my life."

WHEN I SAID GOOD-BYE, the cook from the dining car gave me a bag of food. The porter shook my hand again for the last time. "Take care of yourself," he called after me as I walked away.

Union Station was a huge place, so massive that it seemed that the entire town of Summerton could fit under its roof, and there were large crowds scurrying to the platforms for the trains. In fact, I thought for a while that the station was the city itself. With my mouth agape, I walked around in circles, totally lost. After the long train trip, I had a pressing need and tried to find a restroom. I saw a colored man with a suitcase, walked right to him and asked where the restroom was located.

"Make sure you go into the one that is marked colored," the man said in whispered tones. "You really don't want to get yourself in trouble."

I thought I would not have to see any more such signs after departing from the South, but here they were. Walking through this gigantic structure that had opened in 1907, I could feel the history, the years of people who walked through this legendary structure of Roman architecture just five blocks away from the Capitol. I was only one of a record 200,000 people who passed each year beneath the many arches and vaulted spaces during the World War II years, yet I was determined to make my mark in this city.

"It's over there," a white balding man said as I pointed south. "Look for the sign."

It was a miracle when I arrived in the restroom in Union Station. It was as big as some houses back in Summerton, but much nicer and more luxurious. I inspected the room where the men were lined up to relieve themselves, no hurry, no fuss. The restroom was constructed of white, gleaming tiles with big enamel sinks to wash your hands. This was a new experience for me as I watched the men wait and then use the urinals in an orderly manner. But I acted as though it was nothing new as I stood nonchalantly in the line waiting my turn.

Back in the station, I wandered awhile, trying to get my bearings. The train ride had drained me, and my body was totally fatigued, for it was late in the evening. I looked around and saw some people, both white and black, asleep on the benches, so I found one to stretch out my weary limbs. My eyes searched alertly for any signs of a sheriff or any member of the law. I didn't want to get dragged into the city jail, or worse yet, sent home as a wayward juvenile. Exhausted, I put my flour sack in a corner of the bench, placed my head on it, and fell sound asleep.

A steam whistle blowing loudly woke me up the next morning. I jumped up to find people running past me to hop on a train, carrying their briefcases, as it chugged out of the station. Groggy from sleep, I washed my face and hands in the big restroom, came out, and discovered a secluded spot where I could eat breakfast from my sack of train food.

AFTERWARD, I WALKED AROUND the station until I saw a door with sun coming through the window from the other side. I followed the sun, and before I knew it I was outside staring at my first taxicab. The confusion was maddening, for people of all races were grabbing cabs, going somewhere in a hurry. I searched in my pocket for the piece of paper containing the address my cousin Willie had given me. But I could not find it. I tried to remember whether it said D Street, or F Street, or what.

I stopped a colored cab driver and asked him if he knew my cousin or if he knew where D or F Street was. He reared back in laughter at the country cadence of my speech and the flour sack under my arm. There was no malice in his teasing. I knew that.

"Boy, you're right off the farm, ain't you?" the cabbie asked.

I looked down at my shoes and answered softly. "Yessuh, Summerton, South Carolina. I just got in yestiddy."

"You just arrived in Washington, D.C., the capital of colored America," he proudly proclaimed. "Most folks think they have escaped the South but this is a southern city with everything that they ran away from. We have the biggest colored population of any city in this country. Ever been to Harlem?"

"Nosuh," I replied. I didn't know what Harlem was.

"I was up there once, and Harlem's a colored neighborhood but all the businesses are white-owned and managed," the cabbie said. "See here, this city is segregated but there's a proud, thriving colored community in this town, complete with a middle class. You can work here, have fun here. You can set down roots here. And don't worry about the Jim Crow signs. These white folks and colored folks are never going to say you can't go to this store or that show. You'll just know not to go there. It won't be a big problem, little fella."

I knew all about Jim Crow. I reminded him about my original question about the streets and Willie. The cabbie loved to talk, especially when someone would listen.

"Northeast?" he asked. "Or southeast or northwest?"

I scratched my head, because there were just too many D Streets to choose from. I didn't know which direction the street was going, south or north, or even the neighborhood. Unfortunately, the driver did not know my cousin or where he was. Bewildered, I walked away from the cab, down the strange streets with the sun shining so bright that it seemed to be whitening the gleaming buildings. I'd never seen buildings so high. And then I saw a familiar sight, the Capitol building, looking exactly like the picture of it in my school textbook.

Well, if I couldn't find my cousin Willie, perhaps I could locate the other person who urged me to come by and see him if I was ever in Washington: Senator Burnet Maybank. Upon arriving at Union Station, I'd almost forgotten Senator Maybank while I was so busy learning how to deal with the complicated aspects of this new world.

AS I STOOD on the Capitol steps, they seemed to stretch endlessly, as far as I could see, to infinity. I took them one by one in wonder, leading up to the door, then turned around and looked at the view. The sight was wondrous, impressive with its lush greenery and monuments. I straightened my pants and shirt, and walked inside.

I saw a colored man sweeping up, so I asked him where Senator Maybank's office was located. The man told me to ask the white man in a suit, who was standing nearby, but that man didn't know, so I began asking the same question of every man in a suit I could find. One man said go this way, while another said go that way. I didn't know if I was coming or going. These men had me going all over the building, and after a while I felt lost in a maze, a giant puzzle that had trapped me inside.

However, there was no going back. I had to keep trying. Finally, someone pointed to an open door, and when I looked into the room, I saw a white lady with red hair piled high above her forehead sitting behind an oak desk. She looked busy putting papers in a manila envelope, but that did not stop me.

"Is this Senator Maybank's office?" I asked, still carrying the sack under my arm.

"Yes," she said, smiling. "May I help you?"

The office looked huge to me, with elegant furniture securing the corners of the room, and big paintings of distinguished white men in gold frames hanging on the walls. The redheaded woman—I don't remember her name now, more than six decades later, so I will simply call her "Miss Jane"—listened intently as I told her about how I met the senator back home in Summerton. She was very sympathetic, eager to hear me out, and wrote down my name on a notepad when the telephone rang. I glanced over the desk at a large, black telephone with many buttons. I had never talked on a telephone in my life, so I was very intrigued. I wondered to myself what those buttons could do.

Quietly, Miss Jane finished her call, hung up the telephone, and told me that the senator was not going to be in the office until the following day. I promised I would stop by then.

And I did.

Senator Burnet Rhett Maybank was tall and handsome, with a commanding lilt to his southern voice. He was as cordial to me when I surprised him in Washington as he had been back at McDougal's store. Honestly, I was sure that he did not remember me, and I am equally certain that he was not thinking of me when he issued the public invitation to visit, but I think he really wanted to know all his constituents from South Carolina on a personal level. Southern hospitality meant something then, especially to someone from your own home state. Senator Maybank was an impressive gentleman, about forty-five years old, a man who made me feel welcome instantly, with his ready smile and courteous demeanor.

"What are you doing here in Washington other than visiting me?" the senator asked, leaning against his desk. "Do you have any kinfolks here?"

"Well, I have a cousin, Willie, but I cannot find him," I told him, and then proceeded to make up a story about how I came to Washington on vacation, and wanted a job so I could stay with my cousin.

Senator Maybank nodded. He said he had an idea and took me to the same man I'd seen sweeping the Capitol steps. After introductions, he instructed the man, whose name was Mickey, to look me over. The two of them agreed to hire me to help sweep the steps, giving me suitable employment and a start at a new life. When the senator left, Mickey gave me instructions about the business of sweeping and presented me with a wide push broom with a handle longer than I was tall, and I started working immediately. Standing on those steps every day, looking at the beautiful grounds and public buildings, I knew this was where I wanted to be. I loved sweeping those steps carefully because I just loved to work. I gave my father credit for that. He taught me how to work and how to assess my achievements and be proud of them.

Two of the people who worked under Mickey were named Mr. Walton and Mr. Joe Palmer. Mr. Palmer was in charge of supplies, so I saw him around the building when he put new brooms and mops into the broom closet. I'd never heard the word "closet" before. We never had closets in my family's home down on the farm. We just hung things behind doors and on the bed poles where I grew up. This closet, whose name was a misnomer, was a large room where there were lockers for the staff, tables and chairs, and even a little kitchen in the corner with a hot plate and an icebox.

In one of the room's big corners were mops, buckets, and a huge assortment of brooms, including three different kinds of special ones that were used to sweep the steps. One broom featured a point on the front so that you could get into the corners, and there were portable whisk brooms to carry in our back pockets with scrapers to remove gum and pigeon droppings deposited on the steps. Quite messy. There were brooms for every occasion, more brooms than I ever knew. They had brooms for sweeping the kitchen floor, alcoves, and a special dust mop used on the marble floors.

The first thing Mickey taught me was what broom should be used for what purpose. "We never use a wet mop on the marble floor," Mickey explained. "Even if someone spills something on it, we get the spill up with something special first, and then go over it with a dust mop."

I really didn't know a lot about Mickey. I don't know how old he was when I met him in 1944, the year when America started to turn the tide in the Second World War, but I remember he had been employed by the Senate for thirty years. Everybody turned when Mickey went past—he was tall, about six feet, with light brown skin and straight hair.

Later, I heard that the chief janitor, a white man named Mr. Martin, was sick and that Mickey had been covering for him in that job for about ten years. Mickey loved to talk. He could talk your ears off. He especially loved to tell the story of serving President Herbert Hoover while the president was traveling to the late Calvin Coolidge's funeral. He was so thrilled not only to be one of those chosen to serve the people who accompanied the president and the senators attending the funeral during the long ride to the ceremony, but also have the honor of waiting on President Hoover in person. There was a high tradition of service among these colored men and women, who took delight in being of use to a person of honor or an institution. Mickey was one of these people who loved the esteemed work of service.

For a long time, even while the man was becoming my best friend, I did not know if Mickey had a last name, but I found out much later that Mickey's first name was Talmadge. If you knew what was good for you, you never called him that. Maybe this was because the scourge of the colored people in Georgia was the die-hard segregationist Herman Eugene Talmadge, the state's governor until his death in 1945. Mickey did not like that name in the least. I wondered if he was from Georgia or had relatives there.

Every evening after sweeping, Mickey looked over the steps and complimented me on my work. It was almost a military inspection on his part. I think I deserved the compliments, since I was very diligent and reliable, and watched those steps like a hawk. If one tiny thing fell after I swept up, like a leaf or a piece of paper, I would run to get it and toss it away before Mickey's strict inspection. He was very friendly and talked to me a lot, so I once asked him why he swept the steps with me, since he was the boss.

"If you want something done right, you have to do it yourself," he told me. "Remember that, boy." He advised me on many subjects: work, life, God, responsibility, loyalty, friendship, duty, respect, love, good times, and honor, among them.

He loved to lecture me. "When a senator likes you, like that man do, you best pay attention and stay in touch with him because he will take you a long way. That's how things are here in Washington. Every senator, especially them from down South, will take care of you if you take care of them."

"What do you mean?" I asked.

"If they ask you to sweep, then sweep," Mickey continued. "Don't ask no questions, just sweep. When the time comes when you need a favor, like some more money or keeping your job, that senator will stand up for you."

Sweeping the steps and the halls of the Capitol, you hear a lot of gossip, some good and some bad, but I never heard them say anything bad about Senator Maybank. Although he did not vote the way they wanted him to do, everybody still liked him just as I did. Every time the senator came to the Capitol, he walked over to the steps just to say hello. Day after day, I would rush over to speak to him, and no matter where he was or whom he was talking with, he always reached out his hand and asked me how I was doing.

"Are you doing all right?" the senator asked me in that sweet drawl. "Did you have anything to eat? Is Mickey taking care of you?"

I answered yes to all of his questions. He could see that I was content with my job and my life at the Capitol.

"Come by my office if you need anything," he said. "Promise?"

When I looked into his eyes, I felt that he really cared. If he did not see me for a few days, he would seek Mickey out and ask about me. At the end of every week, I went to Senator Maybank's office and stuck my head in the door to see Miss Jane. I was constantly amazed by her because it seemed she always had on a new dress or a different necklace or scarf. She was a big-city lady, the fanciest-dressed woman I had ever seen.

"Come in, Bertie, the senator has something for you," the lady said. Then she gave me two dollar bills. I thought I was rich. You don't know how happy this made me at the time. Every Friday was payday. Two whole dollars! For me, this was the equivalent of a million bucks, striking it rich. Best of all, she would have it for me every week without fail.

Whenever I saw Senator Maybank in the hall or on the steps, he'd say, "Did you get your money?"

I nodded.

The senator was on the Banking Committee. He constantly talked to me about saving my money. "Now Bertie, I want you to take care of your money. If anyone tries to take it, tell me."

THE SENATOR DIDN'T have to tell me about taking care of my money. I still had my flour-sack pocketbook pinned to my undershirt, my private bank, and I took very good care of it. I thought the two dollars he gave me weekly was my paycheck. Since I had never seen a check or filled out anything indicating I was on anybody's payroll, I did not know the whole process of being a paid employee. I did not know other people got checks every week. He never said why he decided to personally give me two dollars a week, and I never asked him because I thought that was my salary and that the money came directly from the government.

Once when I was in his office, I unhooked the pin from my flour sack and showed him the many dollars I had saved from my salary. I was very proud. It made me feel like I was grown-up.

"Good, always keep some money in reserve and never let anyone know how much you have or where you keep it," Senator Maybank said to me.

Being inquisitive by nature, I learned right away that if I worked in the Senate kitchen, they would pay me off in food, so I washed pots and pans and swept up around the kitchen in my free time. I remember my first time peeping into the Senate restaurant, seeing all the important white people sitting down at pretty tables with white tablecloths while colored men in nice suits served them. To me, it was special, like a picture from a storybook. It looked real elegant.

For the few first weeks in Washington, I went to Union Station to sleep on a bench. I awoke in the morning, stretched my limbs, and hurried to wash my body in the restroom before going to the Capitol. It was my private hotel. But one day after I worked on the steps and the kitchen, I was really tired, and I lay down on some towels in the corner of the broom closet and fell asleep. That was the best sleep I'd had in a long time. It was nice and warm in there, and I slept like a baby.

When I realized it was morning, I grabbed a broom and tried to look as if I was already working. Nobody, not even Mickey, knew I stayed there all night. It was against regulations to bed down in any room in the Capitol unless you had prior approval. The next day, I stayed late and helped clear away dishes in the kitchen, got some of the leftover dinner rolls and a few slabs of roast beef, and ate my late dinner in the broom closet. This time, I got real comfortable and forgot all about those hard benches at the train station where so many people like me slept every night.

Lots of people during the war years had no home. Housing space was limited, with people renting small rooms at a steep price or rooming with families. Some of them hadn't had a home since the start of the Great Depression in the 1930s. Despite the war, which increased the factory jobs, the economy had not yet recovered until several months after the tragic bombing of Pearl Harbor. In some ways, it was made harder because so many common items were rationed. I felt especially lucky to be able to make that broom closet my home for a while. I may be the only person who ever had a "bedroom" in the U.S. Capitol.

Then one day, Mickey came to work very early before I awoke.

"Bertie, we need to talk," he said, looking down at me wrapped in the towels. "Do you sleep here?"

"I . . . I . . . I . . ." I pulled myself to full height and blinked at his towering figure.

He put his hands on his hips and stared at me. "What happened with you staying with your cousin, Willie? If you can't find him we will locate him, because you can't stay here. You staying here isn't good."

I confessed that I never found my cousin because I lost the address of where he lived. Mickey shook his head. The next day, he went with me to Union Station and spoke with some colored cab drivers. One of the cabbies guessed from the address about the neighborhood where Willie might be found. He put me in the car and took me to where Willie lived on 124 D Street S.E., a collection of row houses in a thriving black community. Children ran up and down the street, playing ball and various other games. I kept glancing back and forth along the street, until I saw Willie standing out front talking to some guys.

"Willie!" I called to him from the car. "Willie!"

My cousin could not believe his eyes. He never expected to see me up from the farm, in the big city. He really seemed to be surprised at seeing me. "That isn't you, is it, Bertie?" he said.

"Yes, it is," I declared.

IT TURNED OUT that the guys talking to Willie were also from South Carolina, so I knew most of them. The cab sped off. When I walked with Willie into the house, he introduced the landlady, Mrs. Johnson, an attractive woman wearing a flower-print dress and flat shoes. She informed me that she was from South Carolina and a close relative of Joseph Johnson, a resident of Summerton. I was very glad to meet someone who was from my neck of the woods. Her boardinghouse was in one of the vibrant black areas, a self-sufficient neighborhood where blacks of all economic classes lived side-by-side in the larger segregated city. The place was teeming with quality restaurants, shops, and other businesses owned and managed by blacks.

On the second floor of the house, I saw Willie's room, which he shared with another guy. As I looked around, I was shocked when I glanced at his less-than-fancy clothing hanging in the closet. His shoes were lined up, a bit worn. This room was cramped, although everything seemed in its place, folded and neat. Still, I thought about his Summerton visits, the big house he described in lavish detail, the big shiny car, and the expensive clothes. Immediately, I concluded Willie was a victim of R&B as well, renting and borrowing cars and suits to impress his relatives and the town.

"Can I stay with you?" I asked. It didn't matter that his theatrics for the family were fake—I let all that go since I was so happy to see him. I had missed Willie.

"You have to ask Mrs. Johnson," Willie replied. "I don't think she will have any problem with that."

When I did ask her, she said fine, that I could stay, but I would have to sleep on a bed made up on the floor. A pallet. The fee for my staying there would be two dollars a week. I panicked, for that was my total paycheck, everything the senator was giving me. My mind went crazy with thought. It buzzed with Mickey saying if someone found me sleeping in the Capitol, I would be thrown out of there and he would lose his job. I didn't want that. Also, I wanted to keep my employment at all costs.

However, food was important to me as a young, growing boy. I smelled Mrs. Johnson's good cooking, and then I knew this was the right place for me, a place where I could get cooking with the flavor of my mother's in Summerton. It had been some time since I ate a steaming, delicious plate of good old collard greens, pork chops, and rice with brown gravy. Every morning when I awoke to that aroma of sizzling bacon and grits with a dollop of butter, I agreed to myself that it was really worth my whole week's pay to stay there and eat that wonderful food.

As I settled into the boardinghouse, I started to learn more about the people who lived there. One, the boardinghouse was like home because of the other people from Summerton who had made the journey north to find opportunity. When most of the people left the Carolinas for the "promised land," they were headed for New York, Baltimore, or Philadelphia, yet some of the folks from South Carolina got only as far as D.C. at that time and did not go any farther. Bonding into a tight community of blacks, they piled into this small area of row houses, connected by the hard life that they had left behind, and looked out for each other. It was a true community. If one had food, you had food. If one had a job, that person would get another one a job.

Before integration, the most successful blacks, including the doctors, lawyers, dentists, and teachers, lived in the same community as the maids, butlers, sweepers, and people in the service industry. A large percentage of these people came from the South and knew how difficult it was to be a black person there, so they assisted those late arrivals who were poor and struggling to prove their worth. From talking to the people in the boardinghouse, I understood one thing and that was that everybody wanted to be respected, to have dignity, and to be considered a person of value.

All of these people were a lot older than I was, in their thirties, mature and focused on life. I was only a teenager, full of dreams and notions. The men worked at the Farmer's Market, toiled at Embassy Dairy, and baked at Ottenberg's Bakery. The ladies did domestic work and tended to the children in white people's homes. Most of them stayed in those jobs until they retired. Several people worked a couple of jobs to make extra money, to buy a car, to put away some savings, but they maintained their day jobs and were proud to have them. Nobody had a government job back then, not even cleaning a government building, but everyone had a job, and everybody earned their keep. I never knew anyone who was out of work.

As a teenager, I watched the adults around me and used them as examples, as role models. My cousin Willie, in his twenties, was nearest to my age and constantly wanted to improve himself. Every opportunity was something that he could grasp, whether it was a side job to make some money or to welcome some lovely lady into his life. He was a handsome guy with hazel eyes and a muscular body that girls liked. When he got paid, he started replacing the plain, countrified outfits with the modern, attractive apparel that made the women buzz around him like bees to honey. He liked to go out with them on his days off, getting a car to squire the ladies around to movies and clubs.

I remember one certain woman, very pretty, with long legs, pulling me aside and asking about the kind of man Willie was. "I hope he's not a ladies' man," she said. "I hope he's not one of those guys who loves them and leaves them. Is he?"

"No, he's not," I replied. "He knows how to treat a lady." With that answer, the woman smiled at me, touched my shoulder, and left.

Two days later, Willie stood outside with the guys, joking and talking about life and love. Then he saw me carrying a bag of groceries into the house. He walked up to me, grinned, and slid two quarters into my palm.

"Thanks for the good word to Millie." He laughed. "You're a true friend. I appreciate it, Bertie." We looked out for each other in all things. I knew that he had my back if I needed anything, that he would be there if anything bad would befall me. Now I knew I could go to the movies and see that new John Wayne picture.

THE FALL AND WINTER IN D.C. could be more uncomfortable than at home in Summerton. It was a longer walk every morning to get to the Capitol, with the brisk wind and the swirl of the dead leaves, but not half as long as it was back home when I walked six miles back and forth to school. As the weeks marched toward the end of the year, the weather took a bad turn, getting cold and snowy. It was my first time seeing snow. For a South Carolina native it was a terrible shock, so I was glad to have a warm house to stay in for the brutal Washington winter.

Unprepared for the cold, I still wore my summer clothes, which I'd brought with me from down South. But as soon as it turned cold, the senator gave me a big bag of pants, shorts, socks, underwear, sweaters, hats, and gloves. He slipped me into a large heavy coat, the arms a little long but not much, and said that the bitter wind would cause me to need this coat more often than not. That coat had more pockets than I had ever seen, woven inside and out. The senator told me that the clothes once belonged to the son of someone who worked in his office and the boy had outgrown them. Hand-me-downs or not, they were the nicest clothes I had ever owned. Often, whenever I saw the senator, I'd ask him how good I looked in the clothes.

"Looking good, Bertie." The senator laughed and walked up the steps.

HONESTLY, SENATOR MAYBANK was always interested in helping people, enriching their lives even when he was one of the large cotton exporters in the state of South Carolina before he entered politics. That trait of kindness did not leave him when he became the state's governor, improving economic conditions in South Carolina with a state-sponsored power project on the Santee River. He was a strong supporter of President Franklin Roosevelt's reviving New Deal policies, which rewarded Governor Maybank and the state by making Fort Johnson a major post for the U.S. Army. Politicians in Washington had an eye on him when he was elected in 1941 to fill the U.S. Senate position, having been termed a man of results when he reformed the state's criminal justice system and restored its roads and highways. He voted for federal job programs and public education.

The senator was even concerned with my education, sometimes bringing books for me to read. "Are you reading these books?" he asked me.

I told him yes, even if I couldn't. Reading was not my long suit.

"Bertie, I want you to get with some of the colored boys around here and get them to help you read these books. I know there are some who have been to college. You tell them that I said to help you."

As far as education was concerned, Senator Maybank was a stickler about literacy, writing, and finding a mentor to educate me. "Senator Harrison told me about a man named Jesse, who works for him, going to college. You go see him and get some help with reading."

Seeking out this employee of Senator Harrison, I found Jesse, but he was too busy. Later, I discovered that Jesse R. Nichols was the Senate's first-ever black clerical staff member and a capable assistant on the Senate Finance Committee. Probably I could have learned plenty from Mr. Nichols if he had had the time to meet with me.

When Senator Maybank got back after the holidays, he gave me a small package, all wrapped up with the prettiest paper. Since we'd never used gift-wrapping paper back home, this was the fanciest Christmas present I'd ever seen. I gently took the paper off and inside the box was a brand-new leather wallet.

"Now, you can get rid of that flour sack," the senator said.

We both laughed heartily as I unhooked the flour sack and put my money in my new wallet. He showed me where to put the bills in the billfold, where to put the change. His next question was whether I had a Social Security card, but I didn't. Nor did I have any family photographs, since my family had never owned a camera.

"Here, write your name and address on this paper," the senator said. "If your wallet gets lost, somebody will know where to return it."

This was the test. I knew he wanted to see if I could do it. I wanted to prove to him that I was not illiterate. When I wrote down the information, I could tell by his expression that he was surprised, even impressed. I was not an "A" student in school, but I did learn to read and write, even though some of the books he'd brought to me consisted of larger vocabularies than mine.

Mistakenly, I thought I was the only one who had received a present from my boss, but I discovered that all of the colored people who worked there got Christmas gifts. In a way, I was disappointed. Some received a cash bonus, and many got more than one present. Even the colored women employed in the ladies' room got presents and money. Christmas in South Carolina was never like this, was never as rich as this.

"My new hometown" provided me with a powerful storm of culture shocks, starting with the mesmerizing strings of lights on the various landmarks, monuments, and buildings at night in the city. I had never seen a town so bright after sunset. In Summerton, you couldn't see your hand in front of your face at night, and now I was able to see way across the street in the middle of the darkness. That wasn't all that surprised me. I had never seen so many houses so close together, right on top of each other. This was all right with me, because a neighbor was always nearby. Nor had I seen an apartment house, crowded with families and children, without a fuss. While Summerton's McDougal's store sold everything, here there was a different store for everything, all kinds of specialties: shoes, clothes, and groceries, among other things.

The number of water fountains was astonishing, as was the total of tubs and washbasins in the city. I guess I found it remarkable that you did not have to heat water to take a bath. Hot water came right out of the faucet. A real magic trick. Furthermore, Summerton had few sidewalks or paved streets at the time, maybe because of the high cost of concrete. At home, we swept our yards because they consisted of dirt and rocks, while people had grass in their city yards.

One of my favorite obsessions, however, remained going to the movies. There was a strict color line in the Washington movie houses, with the high-toned white theaters downtown and the black ones on Seventh Street and U Street. Colored folks swore by the quality of everything on U Street—the glow of colored lights on the marquees over its nightclubs, the dance halls, and the private bank it had. The old-timers talked about the style and class of the elegant blacks at the old Whitelaw hotel, the Lincoln Colonnade, and the True Reformers Hall. I never saw so many black people walking up and down the streets, dressed so well, and speaking with such class. My eyes widened as I watched black people driving big cars, eating in grand places—just living in high style.

Everybody spoke of the Howard Theater as if it were a magical place. When I went there with some of the older men living in the city, I saw a large building with balconies, bigger to me with my teen eyes. One of the gentlemen told me that the theater had been used for vaudeville and specialty acts long ago, and he said he saw Duke Ellington, Cab Calloway, Billie Holiday, Honey Coles, Ella Fitzgerald, and plenty of other black stars there. I don't recall any of the musical performers I saw there. All I remember was that it was very exciting.

All that was a big shock to me, but the biggest surprise was discovering that everyday life in Washington was more segregated than in my hometown, Summerton, but it was a different kind of segregation. At home, there were signs that told you where you should be, and we, as colored folks, knew "our place." Up here, I was introduced to what was termed "separate but equal," but it was all divided by race, black and white. Coming from Summerton, where I lived next door to whites, I arrived in a city that was white during the day and black at night and on weekends. When I was at the Capitol during the day, I saw mostly white people except for the black workers, and then I would go home to be around only black people. I was surrounded by people who looked like me, and who, in my mind at least, had "made it." Still, if someone came from the segregated South, he would think the North was heaven, where black people had everything they wanted.

For a thirteen-year-old colored boy, fun was all that mattered. No dreary farm work. This city had everything that could make fun possible: movies, dancing, parties, and places to go and be happy when you were not working. I arrived in a place where black people had fun and got to do more than just work all the time. I thought I had died and gone to heaven.

ONCE I STARTED LIVING with Willie, I knew my whereabouts would eventually get back to my parents, but it took a while. I counted the days and months since my getaway from Summerton. It had been almost two years when Mrs. Johnson, my landlady, called me into the kitchen. She stood in the doorway, arms folded across her bosom, inspecting me as I came into the room.

"Boy, does your mama know where you are?" she asked sternly, her brown eyes piercing mine. "Does she know you are here in Washington?"

Here it comes, I thought. *My Daddy is going to come after me, and I will have to go back to the farm.* I swallowed hard and told her the truth. "Mrs. Johnson, my mama and daddy don't know where I am."

"I just knew you were going to fib," the landlady said. "I was just waiting for you to tell me a lie, boy. I know they been looking for you. Have you been here in Washington all along?"

"Yes, ma'am," I said. I told her how I arrived in the city by Union Station, how the colored people were so nice to me, and how even Senator Maybank had been good to me. I was proud to tell her how the senator gave me a job sweeping the Capitol steps, how I was making good money, but I didn't mention that she was taking all my weekly pay.

There was a moment when she looked me over again. I didn't know what she was thinking. Still, her eyes didn't change their expression of concern and compassion.

"You seem to be a fine, upright boy," she said. "I'll tell you what I am going to do. You might not like it, but I'm going to write your mother and tell her that you are here with me. I also will tell her that I will look out for you. She must be really worried about you. She doesn't know if you're living or dead."

A cold shiver went up my spine. This was the day I had dreaded since my arrival in the city. The landlady must have seen the stricken look on my face, but she continued to explain her plan.

"One thing—will you tell Mama not to tell Daddy that she knows where I am? Promise me that," I pleaded.

In response to my fearful expression, Mrs. Johnson promised me that she would ask Mama not to tell my location. When she got that first letter back from my mother, I was surprised how happy it made me when Mama wrote in her letter: "Take care of my boy." I looked for her to take a vow of silence but she did not say that she was not going to tell my father. However, I did not care by then as I gave it closer thought. I knew that I could find a good place in the city wherever I went, so I was no longer afraid of my father or of him taking me back. Nothing could make me go back to that farm.

As the weeks passed by, Mama wrote me letters on rough notebook paper, which I read over and over with great fondness. I would carry the letters around with me and sometimes read the parts of them that I liked. And then I wrote her back, enclosing a dollar sometimes, which made me feel good. Other guys I knew were sending money home to their mothers. I felt like a real man.

In the meantime, I realized that I needed to make more money in order to provide myself with a decent living. While I no longer needed to wash the pans in the Senate kitchen for food, Mr. Paul Johnson, the headwaiter, sometimes gave me a dollar for helping out. He was always looking out for my well-being, keeping a close eye on my health. I pondered my financial situation, looking for an avenue to bring in more revenue. The idea of getting a shoeshine box came to me one morning when I spotted a guy over at Union Station shining shoes, whose trade was very brisk. White guys were lined up, waiting to have their shoes buffed.

"Mickey, I need a shoeshine box because I need to make some

money," I said. "My debts are starting to get too big. I need to shine some shoes so I can get a little extra money. What do you suggest?"

He looked at me curiously. "First time I've heard of this. If you're serious, you should go down to the carpenter shop. See Mr. Hutman. Tell him I sent you."

At the carpenter shop, Mr. Hutman, the cabinetmaker, and Mr. Jones, his assistant, built all the Senate furniture at the time, all quality materials and design. When I told Mr. Jones that I wanted a shoeshine box, he told me we could construct it together. We tried, but the box never looked right for some reason. Bemused at our lack of progress on the project, Mr. Hutman watched us struggle for a couple of weeks, then he said, "You want a box like that guy over at Union Station?"

"That's right," I said, imagining the all-purpose box.

"Okay," he said. "I'll make you a box that will stand up to some hard work."

In a few days, Mr. Hutman built the best-looking shoeshine box in the world, out of cedar wood, with a top on it with an opening for the cans of polish and brushes and a wooden foot for holding a shoe steady. As a finishing touch, he attached a leather strap to fit over my shoulder. I knew from the masterful job he'd done on the box that Mr. Hutman was a great craftsman, and after that I noticed the pieces of furniture in the Senate that were his creations. Incredible work. Also, I recognized him as a wonderful man to take the time to make such quality equipment for a kid like me.

When I went out of the shop with my shoeshine box on my shoulder, I felt like a professional. Mr. Hutman told me to go to the Senate barbershop and tell them to give me some shoeshine rags, and one can of black and one can of brown polish. Following his instructions, I went to the barbershop and the man shining shoes there, who put ten cans of partially used polish into my new box. He also gave me his old shoe brushes and rags as a bonus. My box was brimming with the stuff he placed into it.

"Watch what I do," the shoeshine man said. "Learn all the tricks. Put some flash into it. Make the brushes perform. Make the rags make music. Make the customer want to come back."

I stayed there awhile, watching him shine shoes. He was a real pro, working the brushes over the leather, making the rags snap over the shoes. He brought out a few pairs in the corner so I could practice his art. In time, I learned a trade that stood me in good stead for a few years, returning to it when I needed some change.

First chance I got, I headed straight for Union Station. While standing on the corner of North Capitol and Massachusetts Avenues, I met my first customer on the first day with my new box. He wore an expensive suit with a white shirt and tie, and put his foot on the box. We talked while I worked on his shoes. A shoeshine was twenty-five cents. He gladly paid it and gave me a tip of a nickel. I shined shoes for about three people, then I had to go back to keep my steps clean.

I could not wait to tell Mickey about my business. "It went really well," I said, feeling proud. "I can make good money shining shoes."

When I did, he quickly told me that cleaning the steps of the Capitol was my primary job, that I should only shine shoes after my working day was over. I promised him that the steps of the Capitol would always be my priority, always be cleaned first. No matter what the weather, whether it was during the hot days of summer or the blustery afternoons of winter, I would do my level best to keep those steps immaculate.

One day, Mickey told me that the senator was asking about me. "You should go see him," he said, knowing that I had been busy with both of my jobs.

I had not seen Senator Maybank as often as I once did, because I had that long walk to the Capitol in the morning. In the evenings, I shined shoes for a growing number of white customers who kept returning to my box, so when I went to his office for my two dollars, I saw only Miss Jane sitting behind the desk. Yes, I was busy, but so was he. I developed a new tactic: Whenever I heard the Senate bell ring for a vote, I would go and stay near the door of the chamber and wait for Senator Maybank. He came running down the hall, carrying important papers under his arm. We exchanged greetings.

"How are you doing, boy?" the Senator asked me. "Are you still saving your money?"

I said yes to everything and he patted me on the shoulder, saying that was good. He was preoccupied with something, some issue or federal agenda. But it seemed like he wasn't there.

Some time around March 1945, there was a big event in the senator's office. When the ladies decorated the room, I asked what was happening, and the reply was that it was a birthday party for Senator Maybank. The secretaries put me to work moving chairs around the room, and then Mickey and some other men joined in to move the heavy furniture. The party started in earnest when several senators and their staff came into the room, laughing and talking, nibbling on the food before they answered the next call to the chambers. After it was over, we went into the office to clean up, sweeping and stacking chairs. The ladies told us we could have the leftover food when we finished, and we took it all down to the basement to have a little party of our own. It may not sound like much these days, but we really appreciated the leftovers.

During our little party, I mentioned to the men that I would be celebrating a birthday soon. They suggested that I should tell the senator because maybe he would give me a cake. I remember talking to the senator about his birthday party, telling him that my birthday was on April 12. He smiled and asked me how old I would be. I really did not want to tell him that I was only going to be fourteen. I didn't know how he would react to that news.

"If you tell me your age, I will tell you mine," I replied, laughing. I had heard that retort back in Summerton a lot.

He just laughed and laughed. I did not want him to know my age because he had once asked me if I had a work permit. I told him no. Although I didn't know what a work permit was, it scared me that he had asked me about that. I asked Mickey about it later, and he said everybody was required to have one. The senator probably thought I was older than I was, since I was big for my age.

When my fourteenth birthday came, I dressed in my best clothes and walked to work. Everything was quiet. No one was around. I went to the broom closet, got my brooms, and started to sweep the steps. On this day, no senators came up the steps. The building and even the streets around it were deserted, more than usual. There was also an unusual sensation in the air, a very solemn mood.

I ran into Henry Young, who was the driver for the Secretary of the Senate.

With a very serious expression on his face, he was rushing up the steps, his body hunched forward.

"Mr. Henry, what is going on?" I asked him. "Is it a holiday?"

He stopped and glanced at me with mournful eyes. "President Franklin Delano Roosevelt has died."

To be truthful, all I thought was: *Why did this have to happen on my birthday? Now I will never get a cake and a party.* I sat on the steps of the Capitol with my head down, despair gripping my heart, and everyone who saw me, thought I was sad for the death of the president. But there I was, feeling sad and distraught because I would not get a birthday cake. It was the thinking of a small-town teenager who was wrapped up in his own wants and desires and not concerned with the world around him. But that was not unusual for a teenager.

That evening back at Mrs. Johnson's house, I told her about my birthday while everyone listened to the radio for the news of Roosevelt's passing. The room was full of men and women from the community, some weeping and others with their sad faces in their hands. I had never realized how much effect the president had on blacks.

As we listened to the radio tributes, one of our residents sneered at the newscaster's mournful voice, saying, "But he didn't end Jim Crow or the lynching of the colored. We still have those signs and can't vote." The others waved him to shut up and continued to listen for any news about the man who had been elected four times to the White House and fallen victim to a deadly stroke just hours earlier.

The radio played an excerpt from a FDR speech delivered on the subject of fear and resolve just seven months before the sneak attack on Pearl Harbor in 1941: ". . . We must not be defeated by the fear of the very danger which we are preparing to resist. Our freedom has shown its ability to survive war, but our freedom would never survive surrender. The only thing we have to fear is fear itself." There were two colored Army men sitting on folding chairs, shouting their pride and clapping. Meanwhile, after dinner, Mrs. Johnson baked me a cake and we celebrated my birthday.

AT WORK THE NEXT DAY, Mickey called a big meeting, saying he wanted the Capitol building sparkling clean for the funeral of President Roosevelt. We knew people from around the world would be coming to our landmark, so the place had to look good. Everyone rushed around to get the work done, sweeping, scouring, and shining every corner and crevice of the building. No one complained. No one asked questions. No one acted as if he did not want to work. We were not like that. Service meant a responsibility to do the job well. We were glad to have those jobs, and we loved what we were doing.

The Capitol had to be maintained in special condition for a long time, for the president was being transported from Georgia to Washington. He was brought across the country on a funeral train under the security of soldiers, and when I heard that they were arriving at Union Station I made it my business to be there. I got a good seat behind a post so that I could see everything. After a ceremony, the soldiers loaded the flag-draped coffin on a caisson pulled by six horses, accompanied by motorcycle escort, for the trip down Pennsylvania Avenue. It was something I will never forget. The whole station was filled to the rafters with mournful people, some of whom were crying.

Slowly, things returned to normal during the weeks that followed as the Capitol service staff went on about their duties, keeping up the grand old building and its grounds. The men often gathered for card games to wile away the time, and the stories sometimes approached the size of tall tales with everybody laughing and joking. These were the times I treasured most with the guys.

"In the summer, down in Virginia, we kids'd pick the bad corn, you know the corn that was planted 'specially for the animals," a strong voice said. We all nodded, waiting for the rest of the story as Theodore Jackson, "Jack" as we called him, picked out a card from the pile and examined the others in his hand.

"Then we went and sold it to white people, sold it like it was good corn!" Jack chortled as we laughed with him. "Man, you could cook that corn all day and all night and it would be still be hard!"

Jack was Mickey's assistant, which meant he and I worked together when the boss had something else to do. Jack was over six feet tall, thin, with glasses, long arms, and big hands. He was probably in his forties or early fifties when I got to the Capitol. A lot of these guys were older than me, and because he was more experienced he took me under his wing in a very fatherly way. He taught me how to be a good janitor and also how to sharpen my card game to be a big winner.

Without a doubt, Jack was the best card player in the basement, a place that did not lack for good card players. He was also a terrific storyteller, although many of his tales felt more like yarns than stories.

TIME PASSED, and I had been working with Mickey sweeping the steps for about two years when he decided we should go downtown to see his cousin in a government office to get me a work permit.

"Now, you're going to have to tell her that you're eighteen," Mickey warned me. I was only fifteen at the time, though I was tall for my age. But the lie was worth it because it was not legal to work without a permit.

We got down to the cousin's office and she gave me a paper to fill out. Mickey made sure I filled it out right. In return, she gave me a card, assuring me that I could work without getting into trouble.

"Keep this with you all the time," Mickey told me. "That way if the police stop you or anybody asks, you got proof that you're old enough to have a job." I went back to the Capitol, swept those steps, and washed those pots and pans with a bigger smile than usual that day, because it felt good to be "legal."

The euphoria did not last that long. One night a month or so later, after sweeping the steps and shining shoes, I went home to settle down to one of Mrs. Johnson's good meals. Her house was very large, with a dining room big enough for everyone to eat dinner and talk every night. She had a table large enough to seat about fifteen people. It was like a big family. Suddenly, all of the South Carolina guys who lived there gathered around the table as our landlady presented me with a letter.

Most of the guys were about five to ten years older than I was back then. All the guys were smiling. Later, they told me that they knew what the letter would say because they had received similar letters long ago in a government envelope just like mine.

"Congratulations," the letter said. "You have been drafted to serve your country." I had no idea what the letter meant, but all the guys in the house knew.

"When you're eighteen, you get a draft notice," one guy explained. "It's Uncle Sam calling!"

Another one stood up and saluted. "You're in the Army now."

I couldn't believe it. "But what about my job at the Capitol?"

"You have to leave your job," a guy said. "The military comes first."

"Come on now, this is very serious," Mrs. Johnson told the guys. "Y'all have to help get Bertie out of this."

"He could get out by going to college," one suggested. "I had two friends back home and they were not called because they were in college."

College, I wondered. *How am I gonna do that when I haven't even finished high school?*

"Or just send it back and say no such person lives here," another offered. "That's what my cousin Billie's family did. When they got his notice, they just sent it back and said that they did not know where he was."

I was shocked. "How did the Army know where I lived?" I asked aloud. "And what made them think I was eighteen years old?"

As the men sitting at the table shrugged, I found myself answering my own question. With Mickey's help I had lied to the government, and that was serious. I reassured myself that if it could be cleared up, Mickey would know how to do it, but I did not sleep that night. That following morning, I got up real early and was waiting on the steps when Mickey got to work. I showed him the letter. We went down to the locker room so he could call another relative, a cousin, who worked at the draft board.

"Well, see, I feel real bad because it's all my fault," Mickey told her. "I need you to do something or else the kid will be in trouble." He put his hand over the receiver and asked me to give him the work permit card. He read the number on it into the phone. They continued talking for what seemed like a long time.

"Come in real early tomorrow," he said to me when he hung up.

A trip to the draft board gave me a case of the jitters. It was housed in a temporary building not far from the Capitol. Slightly nervous as well, Mickey gave me final instructions, telling me not to say anything when we got there. I agreed.

When Mickey's cousin spotted us, she called us to the counter and gave Mickey an envelope. He took it and walked out. Nobody said a word. Inside the car, he opened the envelope and read it out loud. It was an apology, saying simply that the draft board had made a mistake.

"See boy, you don't have to be a senator to have pull," Mickey said proudly as we walked back to the Capitol. "I got pull, too. When they give us these jobs, we have to look out for each other just like the white people do."

I continued to work for Mickey for four more years.

Some time later, Senator Maybank called me into his inner office. "Sit down, Bertie," he said. "I am going to put you on the payroll."

"What payroll?" I asked.

"My friend on the House side needs someone to work in the coffee shop," the Senator said. "And I told him I had just the right person."

"Does that mean that I won't sweep the steps anymore?"

"That's right," he said. "Now you will have a real job and you will be on the payroll." I did not know what to say, because I thought I was already on the payroll.

"You won't have to come to my office anymore for your money," the Senator said. "You will get a check and a lot more money."

AS HE TOLD ME to go for my new job, I said thank you sadly. When I left his office, I should have been happy, but I was not, because I did not want to go to the House side. I would miss the senator. Also, I wanted to continue to sweep the steps.

First thing I did was to go to the broom closet to tell the other guys. They were all happy for me, but I was still sad.

"What's the matter with you?" Mickey asked. "Don't you want to be on the payroll?"

"Well, I guess so," I said.

"Man, the coffee shop is right across the street," Jack said. "You can come over anytime."

They told me that I would be making a lot of money, so I might not have to shine shoes anymore. I didn't tell them that nothing was going to make me give up my shoeshine box. I loved that box so much that when I left to go into the Army, I left it in a locker in the broom closet. When I got back, it was still there and the same polish was inside. I had the same shoeshine box for a long time. Back in Washington, I kept my box on my dresser and maintained its good condition for decades until I finally gave it to a young boy who lived down the street so he could make some money. Now I wish I had kept it.

At the coffee shop, I was a busboy. There were two colored ladies who worked there, one named Mrs. Bessie, and two white ladies. On my first day, I met the supervisor, Mr. Woody, a white man from North Carolina. The House Coffee Shop was right under the House Chambers where the Congressmen worked on legislation. Mr. Woody treated me well. He took me under his wing just as the senator had in those early weeks. Whatever had to be done, I would do it. My duties were to cook hamburgers, hot dogs, and other things on the grill. He also taught me to make lye soap, which we used to wash the dishes and pans. On payday, I got my first paycheck and almost fell down when I saw the amount of money.

Things were also happening for me away from the Capitol. Willie and I moved from Mrs. Johnson's house to live with the Smith family, who owned a big, fine house with plenty of rooms and a basement. One of the Smiths' daughters, Lillian, was active in real estate and fixed up an apartment in the home's basement.

It had a bedroom, bath, living room area, and kitchen, which was the most space I'd ever had to myself since Willie lived in another room upstairs. The Smith family, headed by Edward and Esther Smith, lived not far away from my former landlady, and they had fourteen children, all of the brood older than I. Some were single and living on their own, while others were married, but they still all came by often to visit their parents. I stayed there for almost four years until I decided to save a little money by renting a smaller place in another community. Lillian, the housing agent, found this for me with a family from Georgia. After I moved there, I still considered the Smith family as my family, and I continue to do so. I remain in contact with them and the new generations of grandchildren.

In January 1951 I got another letter from the draft board. The letter did not say "congratulations"—instead, it ordered me to report to Fort Meade in February. I knew I could not get out of it this time, because I was over eighteen. I was working on the House side for almost a year. I went over to tell Senator Maybank that I was drafted, and he was happy.

"Bertie, I am proud of you," the senator said. "I promise you that when you come back, a job will be waiting for you."

Senator Maybank gave me a little send-off party and a gift. Again he wished me well and a healthy return from distant shores. I was very grateful for his friendship and support through the years. But the most satisfying thing was the celebration given for me by the "downstairs" staff, since it was put on by some people I'd gotten to know over the last five years. It was nothing formal. They just stopped to wish me well. As was the custom, there was delicious, hot food cooking on the hot plate in the corner, sodas in the icebox, and groups of old friends laughing at old jokes and memories.

The entire cast of characters was there. George Smith, the Wagon Master (or the head of Transportation), and Louis Queen, his assistant, stood in the crowd gathered where Theodore "Jack" Jackson spun yarns, along with Joe Palmer. Grinning at Jack's tales, "Deacon Strong," a deacon at a local church, almost bent over with laughter. He worked in the file room. Also in the group were Bill Hackney, a driver, and Paul Johnson, the headwaiter in the Senate restaurant, who used to give me free food for washing pots and pans. Everyone knows Johnson as the man who made the famous Senate bean soup, a wonderful concoction the recipe for which people pined but whose ingredients were top secret. Mr. Woody from the coffee shop turned up to celebrate my farewell as well. These people were family, a part of me, and had gotten me through the hard teen years.

Later, just before leaving, I walked through the hallowed building, downstairs and upstairs, and shook hands with people I hoped to see again. However, the last thing was the steps, the Capitol steps, my steps, which had provided me with a living since I arrived in the city. I had to see them one more time. The sun was still bright. The tourists were walking below in the mall, snapping pictures at the monuments. It was my city. It was my Capitol and my steps. Sadly, I looked all around and said a prayer, asking God to please bring me back to this place that I loved so much.

THREE

Growing to Manhood

NINETEEN FIFTY-ONE MARKED THE START OF RACIAL INTEGRATION in the U.S. Army. The Army was the last of the services to integrate, mixing colored with white troops, long after President Truman issued an executive order for the bases to do so in the late 1940s. The order was not given without some pressure from colored leaders, but the man from Missouri rose to the occasion and hasn't been given enough credit for doing such an important thing.

However, the Korean War was the big reason for the Army to finally stop dragging its feet regarding integration, since the bloodletting in combat had left many units without enough white troops to fill in. Honestly, I didn't want to go into the service. War meant bullets, blood, and dying. The newly integrated Army I entered was mostly white. People back then used to say that they did not draft colored recruits because they did not know where to find them. It was a known fact that we did not answer the door when the Census people came by. And, since few of us ran down to the draft board and announced our availability, it took a while for the white people at the draft board to figure out how to find colored folk. Out of the hundreds of people who showed up with me, just a few were colored, and when they divided us up into companies, there were only three or four of us to a company.

The guys sworn in with me at Fort Meade were from Delaware, New York, Pennsylvania, Maryland, and Virginia. These white fellows seemed rich to me because they were all dressed up in new pants, shirts, and shoes with money in their pockets although most had never worked. Their knees were shaking so hard because they were scared to death to be away from home. I was, in contrast, a pro at being away from home. In this group, I definitely came off as a "man of the world," and even older guys seemed impressed that I worked at the Capitol. In truth, of course, the Korean War was raging at the time, and underneath the veneer all of us were scared to death. We just showed it in different ways.

It was whispered that we shouldn't say anything to the soldiers already in uniform with stripes on their shoulders, but I started talking to the sergeant anyway and asked if he needed help passing out the supplies: uniforms, duffel bags, jackets, boots, and the like. He said yes. I liked doing it. I did not want to just sit around like the others and look scared, so I took the advice my mother gave me in one of her letters to keep busy.

On the way to basic training, my group was taken by bus to catch a troop train at Union Station in Washington. We had about an hour of free time before the train was due to arrive. I became a tour guide since most of the group had never seen D.C. before, and I felt like someone special with my insider knowledge. When we walked by the benches where I used to sleep, however, I did not mention that episode in my life.

The train ride to Camp Breckenridge in western Kentucky was extremely long, because the train was not a regular train and therefore had to pull over onto a side track at almost every station to let normal trains go by. These stops took from an hour to a couple of hours each, so the trip seemed to last forever.

And the closer we got to Camp Breckenridge, the colder it got. We all started putting on the coats and boots we'd been issued and tried to eat the rations we were given. In the train, we were handed cans of beans, little hot dogs, vegetables, and corned beef from the kitchen. Then to save time, we were given the cans as a whole meal and were told to open the cans and eat what was in them with a spoon. I did so, closing my eyes and pretending I was sitting at Mrs. Johnson's table eating her delicious pork chops, collard greens, and macaroni and cheese.

At Camp Breckenridge, I encountered the worst winter weather I had experienced in my life, making basic training especially rough. I tried not to shiver and to keep a steady aim on the rifle range. I'd hunted small game like rabbits and birds with homemade slingshots and killed enough that way to keep a steady supply coming in for my mother to cook, but being good with a slingshot didn't help me with an Army-issue rifle. I did not like shooting or most aspects of basic training, but the Army gave us a substantial breakfast every morning, which I appreciated, and I did not mind getting up early.

Despite the newness of the Army's integration policy, all the men in our company trained well together. Of course, we might have been too busy cleaning up the grounds, running with heavy backpacks for miles, and struggling through the mud and barbed wire of the obstacle course while machine guns sprayed real bullets over our heads to think much about racial issues.

After a long stretch of training, you could rate a day pass, and some men used to go into nearby Evansville, Indiana, to let off steam. I preferred to get paid a little extra for doing other soldiers' KP or "kitchen patrol" duties while they went into town and spent all their money. I was young and shy and did not want to waste my hard-earned money on a good-time gal as did some of the others. The women knew what the soldiers wanted and how much they had in their pockets. But I still sent my money to my mother, because times remained hard in Summerton. Also, I did not mind peeling potatoes and sampling the best of the rations in that cozy Army kitchen, where the ovens kept the temperature at a comfortable level.

The month of May rolled around, but the weather still did not warm up much because the sky was always cloudy. Basic training came to an end. All the men looked forward to shipping out. None of us cared where we would have to go, just as long as it was away from Kentucky. My company, the last group to go, left in the middle of the night to head back to Fort Meade, Maryland. The official word was that Company C would get thirty days' leave after being there. They told us that we had better enjoy that leave, because after that we would be going overseas to Korea.

I decided that the thirty-day leave would be a good time to see Mama and Daddy. Many a night in Kentucky when it was really quiet and I was lying in my bunk, I thought about Mama and the joy of seeing her again. For the first time since leaving home, I really wanted to go back to South Carolina. It was time to show my family how I had turned out. I did not know if Daddy would accept me, but I knew a visit from me would make Mama happy.

When the thirty-day leave started, I headed straight for Union Station to catch a train to Sumter, South Carolina, hoping I might get a chance to see the man who had been so kind to me at that station when I had run away.

"The station that was there has been closed a couple of years now," the ticket clerk told me. "But there is a pretty big train station in Florence now, and they have buses to take you to Summerton."

I bought the ticket and sat down on a bench, thinking about the trip ahead. *Would I be able to show my father that I had been successful in life?* I knew he could not make me stay on the farm, because of my orders from the Army. Besides, I was a man now and made my own decisions. I wanted to apologize to my mother for running away, for making her fret about me.

I rode the train as a proud soldier, letting the countryside renew my memories as I gazed out the window. Over and over in my mind, I thought about what I was going to say to Mama and Daddy when I saw them—especially what I would say to Daddy. I was a little scared, but I knew that, deep down, my father loved me and wanted to see me as much as I wanted to see him.

I took a bus from Florence to Summerton, noting that bus tickets had become a lot more expensive than they were when I ran away. The bus stopped at a gas station where colored men with cars were standing around waiting to earn some money by giving people rides. I asked if anyone knew Bob Bowman and they all seemed to, but one man in particular looked me over with a surprised expression on his face.

"I know you," the man said. "You are Bertie Bowman. You been gone a long time, but I remember when everybody was looking for you. I know where your family is. Come on with me. I'm Larry King, your cousin."

Mr. King was the funeral director for Summerton, and he boosted his income by meeting buses with the family car, not the hearse. He was a distant kin to me on my birth mother's side. I suppose he knew just about everybody because of his business, so the news of my disappearance must have been discussed when people gathered for a funeral and then stayed for the repast, the meal after the service.

Stashing my regulation-green Army duffel bag in the backseat, I sat up front with Mr. King. We talked all the way to my father's farm. My life had changed so much, but it had never occurred to me that the country back home might have changed too. "Now *there's* something that hasn't changed," I said as we passed my church, Liberty Hill AME, painted white as it had always been, with the graveyard still full of blooming flowers.

"Oh, changes happening there, too," Mr. King said, "Ask your folks 'bout the school bus."

"Colored kids here got a school bus now?" I was shocked.

"Not yet," Mr. King chuckled. "But coming, maybe."

I saw McDougal's store had closed and asked about it.

"Oh, McDougal?" Mr. King said, "Last year he just closed up and took his family to Florida because his wife was ill. Took everybody by surprise."

I asked about the McDonalds, who were kin to me. Mr. King said they had acquired some new land. Then I saw that the McClary farm and the Hemmingway farm were just the same. I wondered what my old playmate, Bubba Hemingway, was like now.

And what about my family? How much had they changed? The closer we got, the more nervous I was feeling in anticipation of the meeting with my father.

I knew from my mother's letters that my siblings Charlotte, Wilhelmenia, Larry, and Dorothy were still living on the farm, and when we pulled into the yard, Charlotte recognized me and called to the others to come see who was here. I hugged them with joy, and they admired my Army uniform. I was proud of the uniform, probably just as Robert was when he came home so long ago. Then I saw Mama standing in the door. She came running, arms outstretched. We hugged so tight and so long I thought she would never let go.

There were tears in her eyes. I was so happy that I forgot the speech I had planned. All I could say was "Mama, Mama," over and over again while she held on to me. Inside the house, I opened my duffel bag and gave out the presents that I'd brought along, which made them all excited.

Mama and I sat on the porch and talked for a long time. She asked me about Washington and I told her about Senator Maybank and how nice he was to me, and how he said he was going to save my job for me when I got back from Korea. She was very glad to hear that news. We talked about Mrs. Johnson, my former landlady, who by this time had become Mama's old friend.

When I saw Daddy coming from the field, I did not know what to do. My sisters and brother ran to him and said, "Daddy, Daddy, Bertie is home!"

He did not look as though he was glad to see me. His face was expressionless as he walked through the grass. I was very nervous. This was the moment I had dreaded for so long.

"Go, boy," Mama told me, "Go greet your daddy."

As I ran up to him, he grabbed me by the shoulders. "Let me look at you," he said. "You sure are a big boy."

I was embarrassed and cast my eyes down. When I looked up, Daddy was smiling, and I noticed that I was almost as tall as he was. We never hugged. That wasn't his style. Colored country men did not go in for that kind of thing. We walked around the farm, because he wanted me to see what he had done since I had been gone. He had it all running well, with hired men and newfangled machinery from Mr. McClary. He did not ask me about my life in Washington or the Army. He showed me the new barn and the fields, which were flourishing. Then, as we came around the corner of the house, I saw that a shiny Ford automobile was parked there, dark green with four doors.

"See, boy," he said with pride, "this is my car."

My eyes popped wide open because I could not believe it. My

daddy had a car, and it looked fairly new, perhaps a 1946 model. I told him that I'd learned to drive in the service and asked him if I could show him that I could drive.

He said yes, and we got in and drove around the countryside. We stopped at Uncle Robbie's house, and we visited his friend Bill Smyth. For the first time in my life, I felt that my father was proud of me.

He never asked me why I had left home. I suspect he had figured that out, because my siblings told me that after I left he had been easier on them.

One day of my leave, my mother cooked a big dinner for all the family we could gather together. My brothers Rufus and Ernest, who were both in Florida, caught a ride up to Summerton with my sister Bertha and her husband, John, to see me, and my sister Annie, who lived in Summerton, came, too. My brother Robert could not come because he was back in the Marines. I ate all the down-home food until there was nothing left on the table. I really appreciated that cooking after being in the Army with their can rations. To cap off the meal, Mama brought out a big, high jelly cake. I think it was five layers with her homemade jelly between each layer.

Mama was rocking back and forth in her rocking chair under the oak tree in the front yard and I was sitting in the sand in front of her, sipping on the lemonade she'd made for me with a long piece of sugar cane stuck in it because she knew I liked it sweet.

"Some things never change," I told her, thinking back to the many talks we'd had in this very place, and using my free hand to fan away the gnats, which were still ever-present in Summerton. Our talks were very open and honest, and I always felt as though I was special to her.

"Oh, but some things do change," she said, leaning forward. "Remember how you used to have to walk to school every day while the white children rode by you?"

"In their school bus." I nodded. "Spraying us with mud as they went by."

"Well, that is all going to change now, because Reverend DeLaine is working with the NAACP, and they are going to get a bus for the colored children to go to school." Reverend DeLaine and his wife taught at my old school, Scotts Branch.

"Really." I thought back to boot camp. Blacks could be sent to Korea to fight for the country, but black children in South Carolina couldn't have a bus to ride in to school. Some folks still did not know why we were fighting in Korea. Some people wondered why the Chinese were fighting us.

"You know, Ma, a lot of guys up North say they are not going to fight for their country because their country doesn't treat them fair," I said. A lot of black soldiers in Korea had been charged with cowardice, of being yellow, and some of them were said to have resisted orders on the battlefield. The NAACP was checking into the matter.

Mama sighed. "There is not too much in this world that is fair, but just staying away and doing nothing is no answer. We got to band together and everybody scream at once, make such a loud noise they'll have to listen."

"That's what Reverend DeLaine says?"

Mama sat up straight, folding her hands in her lap. "Uh-huh," she said. "They got a piece of paper going around to people to sign, and they say when everybody's name gets on it, they are going to send it up there to Washington where you are. The people from the NAACP say that there is a man up there named Thurgood Marshall? He's kin to the Marshall family over in Goat Island. They're kind of 'well to do.' Anyway, word has it that he will be coming down here to help us get a bus for the colored kids."

My mother was a progressive thinker, always imagining a better future for her children and grandchildren, never wishing them the same fate as she had faced in her life. My mind drifted back to the Capitol steps and my talks with Mickey. I wondered whether Mickey had any relatives who could help us get a bus. He seemed to have a relative in every important office in Washington. I also wondered whether I had ever seen this guy Thurgood Marshall walking the Capitol steps. "When did the school bus thing start?"

"A few years back. Reverend DeLaine and his wife got tired of seeing the children walk so far to get to school. All they asked for was money to fix up a bus so that the kids could ride to school. Levi Pearson took up the fight. His kids have to walk nine miles to get to that school."

"Did he win?"

I had never seen her eyes so focused. "Nope. But a whole lot of people have started getting worked up about it. Nobody's won . . . yet. Whites just got meaner. Punished all the coloreds who stood up to them. That's why we're looking to the NAACP to fight it."

"What does Reverend Richburg say?" I asked.

She stared into space as her mouth got tight. "He thinks Negroes should all stop buying from whites around here. 'You're like mules,' he told us last year. 'You don't know your own strength.' "

"Did you stop buying from them?"

"Not yet." Mama looked away. "Haven't paid dues to the NAACP yet either, but I'm going to. I took some of the money Robert sent me and put it aside to pay. As soon as I can get to one of those meetings, I am going to get financial."

"Financial" was what they said at the church when they were up to date with their payments. "Have you talked to Daddy about joining the NAACP?" I asked her.

"Oh, you know your father," she said, rolling her eyes. "I hear that when he is around his man friends like Mr. Smyth, they talk a lot about what women should not be doing. Your daddy always says: 'What the Pastor says do, the women always do. Men have their own minds.' " She leaned back in the rocking chair. "That is true sometimes but not always."

I stayed around home about a week. Daddy let me use the car to visit my old friends, but I found that every time I asked about someone or stopped by an ex-schoolmate's house, I was told they had "gone up the road." They were getting out of the South in droves. Most of my contemporaries had headed north to New York, Philadelphia, or New Jersey. Either I'd started a trend or I hadn't been the only young black boy dreaming of a life off the farm!

I drove to my old school. The schoolhouse was still the same, but my vision had changed. I was shocked by how primitive it looked. There were just two classrooms—one room for the young kids, another for the older ones—with a potbelly stove in the middle of the floor in each room. Grades one through eight were taught in those two rooms, by about six different teachers. The desks and books were hand-me-downs from the white schools, and many of the books had pages missing. I had forgotten about the well in the back of the school for fresh water, really a far cry from the large water fountains I was accustomed to seeing in public places in Washington.

I can't remember all the things I did on that trip home, but I know I did not work the farm. My father had softened up a bit with my younger brothers and sisters and wasn't as strict with them. They owned bicycles and could go to the movies. They did not have to work as hard in the fields as we had to do. He also gave them money when they wanted to buy candy. I asked Mama about this, and she said that times had changed. She figured that my father did not want anyone else to run away from home. She told me that Daddy always thought that it was his fault that I ran away, and he was trying to make it up to the younger children.

When it came time for me to leave Summerton, Mama gave me the addresses of my brothers Robert, John, and Charlie so I could write them. She packed me a good lunch to eat on the train since colored people were still not allowed to eat in train dining cars.

It surprised me that Daddy and his friend Bill Smyth drove me all the way to Florence to get the train. I remember that the main roads were mostly gravel mixed with tar. There was no line down the middle of the road. Other roads in the town were dirt and clay. If you wanted to pass, the car in front had to pull over.

My father talked about how I should take care of myself in Korea and pay attention and do what my commanding officer told me. He dropped me off at the train station in Florence, and as I waved good-bye I felt as though I had recaptured something very special. I had a family once again.

The trip to South Korea took forever. They bused us to Union Station, where we boarded a train for Fort Lewis, across the country in Seattle, Washington. It was an Army train, and the seats were as plain and hard as planks.

We stayed in Seattle for about a month and then loaded onto a ship that took fifteen days to get to Japan. Most of the men, including myself, were plagued with seasickness. I could not wait to get off that ship. I was like a little kid always saying, "Are we there yet?" After a brief stop in Japan we docked in Pusan, Korea, in the lower part of the Korean peninsula. From there, we rode a train headed for the capital city of Seoul. This train trip took two months, because for some reason it would stop at every little station, loading and unloading for extended periods of time. It was nearly December when we reached Seoul, and winter in Kentucky was warm compared to winter in Korea, which is not that far from Siberia.

Seoul was the last important town before we reached the line where the fighting dragged on with the North Koreans and their allies, the Red Chinese. This front line had not budged much for about five months since peace talks started, but there was no cease-fire declared. The daily conflict was like trench-warfare, where both sides fought little, mostly taking potshots at each other during the day or firing heavy artillery barrages, which might occur at any time without warning. I did not see any real combat action, so I was spared the horrors of the war that had been raging for the two previous years in which bloody battles like Pork Chop Hill had claimed so many lives.

I was in the 32nd Group Engineer Construction Battalion with a man named Colonel Tendy in charge. My job was to pick up the incoming mail, sort it, and take it up to the main line where the combat troops were. I liked my job except for taking the mail close to the front, because the sound of the booming artillery reminded me of the danger. The best part was that all the men were glad to see me because they looked forward to letters from home.

I received a lot of mail myself because Mama wrote to me, as did most of my siblings as well as Mickey and some of the other people at the Capitol. I always saved the letters until nighttime to read and then read them again and again. All of us read those letters from home through many times, since they were the only connection we had to our families and friends. I would read them and then try to imagine what was happening in the world I had left behind.

Mama's letters always came with the usual exhortations: "Stay out of trouble! . . . Listen to older people! . . . Do what they tell you! . . . Don't be sassy!"

But a real drama was playing out in Summerton during the time I was in Korea, and her letters made the drama very vivid, even though I was half a world away.

Something was happening to the grip of Jim Crow in the South. In Summerton, the fight over getting a school bus for the Negro children was getting larger, and more of the community was involved. Mama's first letters said the people were not going to take no for an answer anymore. They were going to fight for the bus. She told me that they had "a piece of paper," a petition, that they were passing around from person to person to get a bus. She also said that if education must be *separate but equal* in segregation, that meant that if white kids had a bus, then black kids should have one, too. In one letter, she told me that my father had told her not to sign but she was going to do it anyway. Another letter reported that she had signed! She sounded very proud of what she had done.

But then, she wrote, things started happening. About a month after she signed the petition, the McClarys, the people we were renting our land from, told her that she had to take her name off the petition. If she did not, Mr. McClary said, he would put the family off the land.

Feeling the pressure, my father told her to remove her name. He never wanted to make any trouble with the white folks.

For a while, she wrote that she was stubborn about her signature and was not going to back down. Then I got a letter saying Mr. McClary started coming up to the house every night to ask her if she had taken her name off. My father told her the family would not have anywhere to live if she did not do it, because the white people owned all the land in the county.

Then came an emotional letter in which Mama said she felt she had to take her name off the petition, but she stayed involved in the case. She wrote she was "beaten but not bowed," for my mother felt she was right. The fight, she predicted, was going to go across the country because more colored parents would demand equal education for their children. She realized that getting a good education was the best asset for the future of our young. Over my father's loud protests, she kept going to the meetings at our church.

There were very few blacks in my division in Korea, but this was a subject we whispered about excitedly when we got together by ourselves. Could it be that things were changing back home? Everyone wanted to know what was happening in Summerton. This was also something we did not talk about with the white guys, since we did not really know who was in favor of integration and good race relations.

When I was overseas, I sent my mother an allotment check every month. I knew that my brother Robert used to send her some money, too, but since Robert was now a married man he probably needed his money for his own family. My mother wrote about how much she appreciated the money because Daddy had become ill and could not farm anymore. I never knew what was wrong with him—no one did since there were no black doctors or hospitals in our town in the late 1950s—but I was really glad to know that the money I sent helped out my family. To be truthful, I am not sure that I would have gone home to see him even if I was permitted to go to Summerton. I loved my father but my feelings for him were not the same as those for my mother.

"You are a good boy, Bertie," Mama wrote in her letters. Daddy never wrote me, but Mama would always write: "Daddy says hello."

In October 1953 we got back to the United States and I received an honorable discharge from the Army in November.

The very next day I went back to the Capitol to get my job back. Senator Maybank welcomed me heartily, and we talked for a long time about my experiences in the service. I had matured greatly in the time I was in the military. I was no longer the shy, bashful boy that he'd first met. There was a change in how he treated me, like a grown-up.

"Now would you like to go back to the House side, or do you want to come over here again to the Senate side?" he asked me after we'd talked for a while.

"The Senate," I said, remembering the good times.

"I have to tell you, Bertie, there's a job on the House side that would pay more."

"No, I've always been more comfortable on the Senate side," I told him. "This is where I started. I can't explain it, but I always feel good walking the halls of the Senate." I shrugged. "And you're here."

He smiled and patted my arm. "Then the Senate side it is. Go see George Smith, the Wagon Master, or his assistant, Louis Queen. Welcome back."

Within minutes I had met with both men and was hired as a janitor, my first substantial job on the Senate side. It was good to be back home, around good friends and good memories.

Before starting the Senate job, I took a quick trip back home to Summerton. This time when I walked into the Hemmingways' store I ran into my childhood playmate, Bubba Hemmingway, the sweet but uncoordinated white boy next door whom I'd let win at kick ball every so often just to keep things interesting. He was all grown up and seemed a bit sullen.

"Hi, Bubba!" I said excitedly when I spied him standing behind the counter alone in the store.

He seemed startled by my sudden appearance. I decided maybe it was my military uniform, or the fact that I was now much taller than he. Yes, Bubba had changed too and not for the best. He was fat and balding, but surely after all the time we'd spent together we were both recognizable. It hadn't been *that* long ago.

"It's Bertie, Bubba," I said warmly, holding out my hand.

He shook my hand quickly. He looked me up and down and then glanced around to see if anyone else was in the store. "Bertie," he said, clearing his throat while doing a little dance of shifting uncomfortably from foot to foot like he might wet himself. "Around here now, everyone calls me Mr. Hemmingway."

A chill crept up my spine. *Had he heard that Mama had signed that petition and did not want any of his family to even see him talking to me? Or was it that now we were adults and black and white, rather than old friends?* It was as if that same old poison of hate had seeped into the body of my old pal, changing him into somebody I did not know.

"In Washington, D.C., at the United States Senate, everyone calls me Mr. Bowman," I said, maintaining the smile on my face.

He turned red all over, even his ears. But his eyes had an evil stare that I knew all too well from when certain whites looked down on their colored help. As if I were an inferior person.

I looked him straight in the face, turned slowly, and left, slamming the screen door so hard I heard canned goods falling off the shelves. That behavior was not something I was going to accept, not then or ever.

UPON MY RETURN, I settled down to my work. In the Senate janitorial service, we all had regular chores to prepare for the day, and then we were available to work for any senator who needed us. I was extra-available and got teased a little for my enthusiasm. I was the youngest on staff and the most anxious to see as much of the upper floors as I could, for the upstairs, after all, was where the real action was. Whenever we got a call from a senator's office, I was first to jump up and answer the phone.

The older guys were only too happy to stay in the basement and keep playing cards. Theodore "Jack" Jackson was still the best card player in the group, and still a constant storyteller. Jack loved to tell us stories about how he and his buddies had outsmarted all the white military men when his family lived across from the Washington Navy Yard.

"They had a big horn up on the roof," Jack began telling his yarn. "You know, the kind that made noise when it was time for the sailors to get up in the morning? Well, a bunch of us climbed up one night onto the roof and put gravel into the horn, and the next day the sounds came out all muffled."

He shook his head as he checked his hand. "We watched it all from our window and laughed. Oh, how we laughed."

"Oh, come on, man, where were the guards?" someone asked Jack.

"Yeah, how could you get on the roof without them catching you?" another questioned. They always wanted to trip him up but he was good at his tall tales.

"We were too smart for them," he said proudly. "Just too smart."

I was still laughing when I entered the senator's office. "I'm hearing good things about you, Bertie." Senator Maybank leaned forward in his office chair and looked intently into my eyes. "You're a hard worker, reliable, dependable. People like that. But remember what I told you."

I knew it by rote. "That I need to look, listen, and keep my mouth shut?"

"That's right. The key to doing well here in the Senate is to be seen as trustworthy. You need to pay close attention and remember what you hear and see, but discuss it with no one. And no one means *no one*. If a senator knows he can trust you to keep to yourself whatever you hear or see, he'll rely on you."

This was our pre-holiday visit, because the Senate was about to go into recess for the next five months, from July through to January, but just about every visit began with fatherly advice from Senator Maybank. He seemed more relaxed than usual today, with his white shirtsleeves rolled up and without a jacket. There were papers on his desk, awaiting his attention, but I guessed vacation was on the horizon.

"Are you going to Flat Rock during the recess?" I asked. He had a summerhouse in the mountains of North Carolina, and he'd often talked about how much he loved spending time there.

"For part of it, yes." He sighed as he relaxed in his chair. "I can't wait. Can't tell you how much I'm looking forward to sitting out on my porch and watching the sun go down in the evening and taking in that nice breeze that comes down from the mountains." He sat still, as though picturing it for a golden moment. "How about you? How is your father feeling?"

I felt sad for a second, then replied. "Mama says he's still too sick to do farm work. I've been helping out a little, sending money."

"Good for you, Bertie. Are you going down there for a visit?"

"Maybe later," I said. "First, I was thinking of taking on a few odd jobs to earn some extra money." Recess meant that Senate employees like me had five months of light work, and no work with full paychecks on some days.

The senator smiled. "That's the idea. More money for the savings account." Save your money and prove yourself trustworthy were the recurrent themes in Senator Maybank's advice. I followed both religiously.

In time, I was working an extra job, sweeping up at Griffith Stadium before the Washington Senators' games and had brought my little portable radio with me to ease the monotony and boredom.

Suddenly the music was interrupted by a news bulletin. *"South Carolina Senator Burnet Rhett Maybank died suddenly today of an apparent heart attack at his summer home in Flat Rock, North Carolina. He was 55. . . ."*

I was shocked. I had never before had someone close to me die. I kept remembering how he'd looked the last time we'd talked—so healthy and active. It really shook me.

Instinctively, I went to the Capitol as soon as I'd finished at the stadium. Everyone there was talking about it. I went to Senator Maybank's office, only to find the door locked.

I listened to the news. The funeral was going to be in Charleston, South Carolina, his hometown. I wanted to go—in fact, I had to be there.

"You got people in Charleston?" Jack asked me.

"No," I replied.

"You know anyone with family in Charleston?"

"No."

"Then how you gonna go down there?" He had a worried expression on his face.

He was right. Back then, hotels were not open to blacks, and if you didn't have a friend or relative to stay with there was no way to visit a city. Jack even asked his guys around in the basement for me to see if anyone had relatives there who could give me a place to stay. But with no luck.

A chartered plane of senators and other officials from Washington was going down to the funeral, and there was to be a ceremonial motorcade in Washington to the airport and back. I was called and asked to drive the Secretary of the Senate, Skeeter Johnson, and other Democrats in the motorcade. This was both flattering and gratifying. It made me feel that I was participating in the final farewell to Senator Maybank.

And, of course, I loved the idea of chauffeuring people around in a big shiny car, just like the chauffeurs I'd been awed by in my youth outside the McDougal store in Summerton.

I got all dressed up, went to the Senate garage and polished the car.

The procession was long and involved Supreme Court Justices and State Department officials as well as members of Congress. When Senate Minority Leader Lyndon B. Johnson arrived in the garage, a large group of Democrats gathered around him, strategizing about how the party might hold on to Maybank's seat. The talk was brisk and lively.

The conversation continued in the backseat of the car I was driving, along with a debate on who would be the best person to replace Maybank. I found this talk disrespectful. The man wasn't even buried yet! But adhering to my mentor's advice, I listened attentively and kept my mouth closed.

We all stood at attention at our cars until the plane took off. I used that moment to thank Burnet Rhett Maybank silently for all he'd done for me.

Since we were all due at the airport when the entourage returned from Charleston later that night, there was a lot of downtime. I loved hanging out in the Senate garage with the drivers as they polished and re-polished their cars, listening while they talked about politics. None had college degrees, few had high school diplomas, but all were very knowledgeable when it came to politics. They let me listen but never expected me to participate in their conversations, because they felt I was too young to know anything. To underscore that point, they all called me "Youngblood." Most of the guys were about twenty years older than I was at that time.

I looked up to them because most had been driving senators around for years. The drivers had a little waiting area where they sat around and ate and talked. When you were not driving, you took care of the car. There was competition, with everyone trying to "out-shine" everyone else. One was a tire expert, for example, and he would show the other guys how to make those wide whitewalls really look good.

Many of the chauffeurs liked to drive the cars into their neighborhoods after they dropped off the senator instead of coming right back to the garage. They wanted their buddies and their girlfriends to see them driving that big, pretty car.

All the drivers were black. It was a known fact that senators did not want whites driving them. Somehow they felt that they could do, say, or act any way they wanted around blacks and blacks would never tell.

As we waited at the airport for the return flight, they were busy pooling information about the race to find a successor.

Someone put out the obvious. "They don't even have that man in the ground good, and they got three or four people in South Carolina going to a secret place to talk about who they gonna nominate!"

"Governor Edgar Brown already has it," another one said. "Everyone says."

The first chauffeur was adamant. "Uh-uh. No sir. I don't know who you think "everyone" is, but all the fuss is because they don't *want* him to get it."

This was a very important seat, since Senator Maybank had been a shoo-in for re-election but now nothing was certain. The Republicans in 1954 enjoyed a majority in the Senate but only by one seat. With the election coming up and such a small majority, one or two seats could make a huge difference. I listened and learned.

When they weren't talking politics that night, they were worrying aloud about me. Who was I going to have in my corner, now that Senator Maybank had died? Every one of them had at least one senator who looked out for him.

About a month after the funeral, they held a memorial service for Senator Maybank in the Senate. Mickey gave me the day off, and the doorkeeper gave me a special seat in the Senate Gallery so I could listen to the speeches. First, they said a prayer, and then senator after senator got up to say lofty things about Senator Maybank, usually in very flowery language. I looked around the gallery for Miss Jane and the other members of Maybank's staff, but they were not there. I realized how temporary employment on the Hill was. With their senator no longer in office, they were all back in South Carolina or elsewhere.

Meanwhile, the debate among the chauffeurs and the downstairs help continued with a frenzy. Everybody had an opinion.

"I told you no one wanted that Edgar Brown guy!"

"How come he got the nomination if no one wanted him?"

"Brown was the governor of South Carolina!"

In the end, Edgar Brown, the Democratic nominee to fill Senator Maybank's seat, lost the election to a write-in candidate, and everyone in the locker room was buzzing about the winner, J. Strom Thurmond.

"They say some people in South Carolina just wrote in 'Strom' because they couldn't spell 'Thurmond,' " somebody said.

"You can win that way?" I wondered aloud, "I could just write my own name on the ballot?"

"You can write your name on the ballot." Jack laughed. "But unless a whole lotta *other* people write it too, you're not gonna win."

It was a kind of "guy" thing. This Strom Thurmond had fooled everyone by beating the sure winner in a write-in vote, and that's the kind of surprise men love to see in any sport. It was the political equivalent of faking a throw in football that leads to a touchdown or shocking a batter in baseball with a sudden change-up pitch, or surreptitiously feeding a teammate the basketball from behind your back that leads to a winning basket. Strom Thurmond, the underdog, had fooled everyone by doing something we'd never heard of before, winning a statewide election by a write-in vote, and we were all dying to see what this guy who had done something so clever looked like.

As a result, everyone from the basement was volunteering to help get Senator Thurmond's room together just so they could get a look. No one cared much that he was a segregationist. We were used to them. There were a lot of those in the Senate back then. It was a while before we knew how *much* of a segregationist Strom Thurmond was, but in the early 1950s, people, especially senators, were saying all kinds of hateful things back home in order to stay in office. They knew what their people wanted to hear and they gave it to them.

And, truth be told, we black Senate employees did the same thing. We knew what our senators wanted to hear from us and, to get a raise or a better job, we gave it to them. It wasn't Uncle Tomming but survival. We knew the game. At that time, the big paychecks we received were more important to us than what any given senator said when he made his campaign rounds.

Don't get me wrong. None of us bowed and scraped. But, I did say "no, sir" and "yes, sir" because I was a southern boy with good manners.

And good southern manners cut across racial lines back then.

"Hello, Mr. Senator," I said to Strom Thurmond, the first time I saw him in the hall. "I'm Bertie Bowman. Senator Maybank was a good friend of mine."

Thurmond smiled warmly. "He was, was he?"

"Yes. I'm from Summerton, South Carolina."

"You still got people down there?" he asked.

"Yes, I do, sir."

He tapped me on the shoulder. "Well, then, Bertie Bowman, you let me know if they need anything," he said, "I'll take care of them."

The next time I saw him, I asked him if we could have a talk. His staff arranged time for me, and we talked a long time about South Carolina and Senator Maybank. From that day until he died, Strom Thurmond and I were friends. He invited me to office social events and always respected me as a person. There was never a time when we passed each other in the halls that he did not stop talking to the person he was with to say hello to me.

He also kept his word. Whenever anyone in my family needed something where a politician could assist, all I had to do was tell Senator Thurmond and he would get a staff member in his home office to see to it. The word got around Summerton that Negroes were listened to when they went to Thurmond's storefront office in Manning, South Carolina, and many families went there to get the personal things they needed. He was a typical southern senator back then. Politically, he fought against civil rights and gave his segregationist voters what they wanted to hear. Personally, however, he was someone Negroes could turn to for help.

At that point in time that was all Negroes could expect from a senator.

The Downstairs Crew

M EANWHILE, THE CAPITOL'S DOWNSTAIRS HELP REALIZED THAT the "times were a-changin' " for black folks not only in the Deep South but in the country as a whole. I really didn't know what to make of this trend. I never thought the South would change. The guys, Oscar Quarles, Norman Scroggins, Johnny Price, Louis Queen, Ernie Montgomery, and I were all sitting around eating lunch in the basement and discussing some of the articles in *The Baltimore Afro American,* one of the most popular black newspapers of the day. Jack Jackson bought it religiously every Tuesday and Thursday, because those were the days the paper featured political cartoons by "Ollie" Harrington, which he let us all read, providing we didn't mess it up.

"See this?" Jack asked. He held up the political cartoon he'd just cut out. It pictured Thurgood Marshall, the chief NAACP lawyer, sticking his head out of a train.

We all nodded, although some of us didn't have any idea what it meant.

"This isn't one of those funny cartoons," he said. "It's got meaning."

We all nodded again. Nobody wanted to appear dumb.

"So, what does it mean?" he asked us. "What does the cartoon say?"

Suddenly, the room got quiet as six guys stared blankly at the cartoon.

"Dunno," someone finally mumbled.

"See how the train's moving?" Jack said, pointing, "Thurgood's *driving* that train, man. It means he's won that case and taking us all with him! Black kids, white kids, all going to the same school, learning the same thing."

We all knew about that case, the Supreme Court decision on *Brown v. Board of Education* in May, which opened the door for the end of segregation in public schools. The decision showed that Mr. Marshall was a man to be reckoned with. It meant the end of Jim Crow, or so it seemed. But many black folks knew it would take more than a court decision or a paper being signed to change the minds of some of the white people below the Dixie line.

Walking briskly, Jack stood up and moved over to the corner, shaking his head as he tacked the cartoon up beside many others. "Thurgood Marshall's gonna be the baddest colored man in this country!" He chuckled. It was a prediction Jack had been making since Mr. Marshall came on the scene in 1954. The guys loved to look at the corner with its political-cartoon gallery—drawings showed off his serious side, but he could be so funny when he wanted to be.

I thought about the news I was getting from Summerton. My mother wrote me that they were dancing in the streets, or more likely on the farms, when the news about the Supreme Court decision reached them, but then things became quiet and no one knew what to do next. A lot of white businesses closed. There was a troubling calm. People, white and black, stayed in their homes, sensing something was going to happen. Nothing did.

Soon after, the white schools closed, and for a while, no one could figure out where all the white kids had gone. It turned out that they opened several private schools, with some schools even in churches so they would not have to mix with the colored kids. It was a surprise when black folks started seeing a new school being built. When it opened, the blacks lined up at the door and they all went there, along with the poor white children from the trailer park. This was Summerton's version of integration. The "well-to-do" whites continued to go to their private schools, while the poor, both black and white, went to inferior schools, so Thurgood Marshall's train still had a way to go.

Everyone, black and white, who came into our locker room went right over to Jack Jackson's corner and read those cartoons. Sometimes we understood them, and sometimes we didn't. The white guys never commented on the cartoons. They just read them. Gradually, there got to be so many cartoons that there was no more room in the corner. Jack then bought a scrapbook. This enabled him to not only paste his cartoons in one place, but to write comments about them. That scrapbook was his prized possession. He enjoyed writing in it so much that I caught the spirit and went out and bought a diary and began making regular entries of my own.

Skeeter Johnson, the Secretary of the Senate and boss of all the support staff, including us, would come in every so often and say, "Hey, Jack, let me see that scrapbook of yours."

"Don't have it here today," Jack replied, sometimes even with the book sitting right there. "It's not here. I took it home."

Graciously, Skeeter let it slide. He was Jack's boss, but he never messed with him. A rough-looking, tough-talking white man from Mississippi, he was referred to as "the Wolf" behind his back by many of the blacks on staff. Skeeter Johnson would give you the shirt off his back if he liked you, and would force you to work Saturdays and deny you days off if he didn't. I made sure he liked me.

I first got to know Skeeter by driving him to the airport in the procession for Senator Maybank's funeral. After that, I began driving Skeeter and his wife to Senate and White House functions, and gradually got to know them well. It was amazing to me how much you could learn about politics and how many friendships you could forge by sitting at the wheel of a car.

With time, I moved up through the ranks. I gradually progressed from being on the Sergeant at Arms' payroll to joining the Secretary of the Senate's payroll. That was a big thing. I was still doing some janitorial work, but I was no longer wearing a janitor's uniform, with more contact with people in other parts of the Senate.

I was a student and the Senate was my university. The more I knew, the more I wanted to know about the workings of the place, so when someone was looking for someone to do something, I usually volunteered.

I loved working in the Senate Library. For example, when I helped stack the shelves, I learned the system and thus had an easy time finding things when necessary. At that time, the book binding was done in the Senate Library, and when I finished my regular duties, such as delivering research work and congressional records to the senators' offices, I was often asked to help the book binder.

Books were bound one book at a time and by hand. The *Congressional Record,* the *Senate Report,* hearing testimony, committee hearings, bills, resolutions—all were printed at the Government Printing Office and sent to the Senate Library to be bound. The pages of the book were sent down to the library with a rubber band around them. We'd wrap the pages with a cord, glue the back of the pages, and then glue that to the hard cover. The book was then put in something called a "bit," a contraption that held the pages together tightly until they dried. They stayed in the bit a day or so until the binder told us we could take them out. Then a title was put on them, and we loaded them into boxes.

Back in the narrow halls of the Capitol, Senator Wayne Morse, an Independent-Democrat from Oregon, was causing quite a fuss. And a stink as well. The senator raised prize bulls on his Maryland farm and entered the Senate every morning with foul-smelling manure on his shoes. As was his custom, he came straight to the bath, a luxurious oasis of comfort that had been created for the lawmakers in the 1800s, when most of them lived in boarding houses on Capitol Hill without adequate bathing facilities. The Senate bath had exquisite facilities, with a hot tub, showers, a sauna, a swimming pool, and individual robes for each member of the Senate.

And, most mornings, Senator Morse took advantage of the bath. He took off his manure-laden boots and gave them to Mr. Henry, who dumped them into a bucket with detergent and washed and polished them up for the senator. When they noticed the manure had gotten on the senator's pants as well, Francis Coles and George Todd cleaned them for him, but the senator still rarely noticed the odor himself.

On this particular day and some others in the past, Francis and George had been busy doing other chores, so they neglected the bad-smelling pants. As a result, the senator had left the bath still reeking of manure.

"He's gotta be the *smelliest* senator!" someone said of Senator Morse.

"I'll say!" another guy replied.

"You got that right!"

"He don't have to make noise for you to know he comin'!" The first one laughed.

All the guys in the locker room cracked up.

"Well, it's not the boots," Mr. Henry insisted, "I washed them real good."

Mr. Henry, Frances Coles, George Todd, and occasionally I were part of the Senate's downstairs staff. We cleaned up offices, helped man the barbershop, shined shoes, and kept the beautiful tubs and showers of the Senate bath shining. We were all black, and we all worked in service jobs as laborers. The electricians, painters, carpenters, and plumbers—all of the skilled employees who worked in the Senate—were all white. When they needed help painting an office or a hearing room, for example, they would call from upstairs for assistance from the downstairs employees, the janitors. The painter only painted the walls. It was the downstairs laborer who carried the jug of paint, brought the painter the brush he requested, and cleaned up the mess when the painter finished painting.

We downstairs employees also cleaned up the senators themselves, since we staffed both the barbershop and the Senate bath. This meant removing not only manure but other telltale stains and scents, dyeing their hair to make them look younger, and putting lifts in their shoes to make them look taller. All the cosmetic things.

We thought of ourselves as the "invisible workforce," because the senators carried on as though we weren't there, saying things out loud that would ruin a political career nowadays. It was as if we were chairs or tables. They compared notes on devious plans to take land away from poor people in their home states who had not supported them and were behind on their taxes. Then they devised ways to have their friends and relatives pay the taxes and seize the land. They conspired aloud about how to tack on provisions to benefit rich contributors to bills on the Senate floor, which was called "pork."

What amazed us most of all was their lack of decorum. These men, who could charm voters and deliver flowery orations on the floor of the Senate, let go of all social graces when they came to the bath. They cursed, told dirty jokes, said nasty things about each other, passed gas, and, if they wanted to use the "N" word in front of us, they did that, too.

Uttering a racial slur while surrounded by black employees would be shocking in today's world, and so would the amount of scandalous information they imparted while we just kept working around them, pretending to be as oblivious to what they were doing as they seemed to be to our presence. Like I said, we were invisible.

It was only later, at quitting time, when we were alone together in the locker room that we told tales and hooted and howled at some of the things we'd seen and heard. Some things disgusted us, but very little surprised us. We knew their personalities, the assets and flaws of the lawmakers. We usually knew who was going to vote how before a bill came up on the Senate floor. We got our information well in advance of the newspapers, just by listening as they sat in the barbershop cajoling, fighting, sometimes even jumping out of their chairs and screaming at each other in their attempts to convince fellow senators to alter their votes.

"I'll give you this, if you give me that." It sounded like kids trading marbles, but instead it was one senator offering to tack on a provision to raise the pay for the military in exchange for another senator's adding on an amendment to pay farmers more money for not planting corn. And sure enough, a week after one of the guys in the locker room told us about the trade-off he'd overheard, we'd read in the newspaper about the "last-minute compromise" enabling the bill to pass into law. We were listening to history in the making. Most Americans would not believe serious national issues were decided after a heated argument in adjoining barber chairs.

We were privy to information that never made the newspapers, too. Hot gossip flowed from the barbershop and the bath directly into the locker room of the "invisibles." When General Eisenhower was president in the late 1950s, the barbershop was full of talk about his girlfriend, the attractive young Army captain he'd met long before he became the chief executive. In Washington political circles, both Democrats and Republicans knew that she was in and out of the White House all the time without Ike's wife, Mamie, even suspecting.

While most senators whispered about the president's affair, Majority Leader Lyndon B. Johnson, the Texas firebrand, talked about it out loud, much the way he talked about his own affairs. No one generated more locker-room gossip and speculation at that time than Lyndon Johnson, because he was so powerful in his leadership post and so hated by the other senators. His personality had a larger-than-life quality.

He was conversation-topic number one in the Senate barbershop. We got a kick out of the fact that everyone bad-mouthed him, but everyone was terrified that he'd find out. I remember once when I was sweeping up the barbershop and a group of senators were complaining about all the things Johnson was doing that they did not like. One of them suddenly hushed the crowd and turned to the Page twins, who worked there as downstairs help. "One of you stand inside of the door and one of you stand outside the door," he instructed them. "And when you see that big-foot senator from Texas come up the hall, let me know!"

We loved watching the lawmakers fawn all over him when Johnson came to get his hair cut. The anger was quickly transformed into a love fest, with any senator who was present yes-sirring him, nodding his head like a heifer chewing a cud, and patting Johnson on the back.

Johnson usually saw through the act. "I know you were talking about me before I got here," he said to the guilty party. "But I don't give a damn."

We all felt that Johnson got the biggest kick out of letting people know that he knew that they did not like him. He also liked to curse and scream at his fellow politicians and demonstrate his acute ability to hear through the walls.

"I know you want that highway construction package put back in the transportation bill," he yelled, "but goddammit it ain't gonna happen!" And the same senator who, just a minute before, was conspiring to get the construction package put back in for a vote would swear that was the *last* thing on his mind.

"Well, then," Johnson said. "I better not hear about you bringing it up in Committee." And the senator would leave the shop like a kid who had just been scolded by his father.

We Invisibles loved having Johnson around. We loved to see those other politicians squirm. When Johnson was in charge of the Senate, you did what he said or you did not last long. Somehow, anyone who opposed him would get defeated. Sometimes we took bets on which senator would be back after an election. "Mess with Johnson," we used to say, "and you can kiss your seat good-bye."

As a senator, Johnson spent a lot of time in the barbershop, because he loved to be "decked out" like a well-dressed cowboy. Like his fellow lawmakers, we, of course, were also driven to make the Senate Majority Leader happy. Two downstairs workers, Willie Lewis or Jimmy Carter (no kin to President Jimmy Carter), would run to get him an ice-cold Fresca, a popular soda drink, as soon as he walked in. One hoped it was before he howled: "Where in the #~!@!## is my Fresca?" No one cursed as loudly and creatively as Lyndon Johnson. He loved food, especially "Texas cooking." He told us that his cook, Mrs. Wright, made the best popovers in the world, which he called as "smooth as a baby's bottom." Knowing he loved peach ice cream, I'd usually go down to the restaurant while the guys were struggling with the Fresca and get him a generous helping.

"Bertie, this peach ice cream tastes like you went out back and picked the peaches right off the trees," Johnson gushed with a toothy smile that could charm birds out of the sky.

Johnson might have had a nasty side to him, but he tipped very well.

DID WE INVISIBLES FEEL like "house" slaves working on a plantation? Yes and no. We certainly did feel like servants, but we were well-paid servants. The downstairs employees in the Senate had better jobs, sick leave, salaries, days off with pay, and retirement benefits than they would with just about any other jobs blacks could get in Washington at that time. When I ran away from home, all I wanted was to be somebody. I wanted my own freedom. Although I didn't have much book learning, I had a perfectly working mind with which to think things over. I never made a step before looking first.

Somebody once told me that a man only truly lives as a man when he knows the truth about himself. I am a simple man without pretenses. All I wanted was to grow up and grow old in a world that didn't make too many demands on me. At this point in my life, I was always pleasing somebody else. I tried to find a kind of peace and contentment in the work of making others happy. Like a lot of southern black men, I learned to live without watching myself live and to work without expecting a fast, quick reward.

Now some folks would say I was a servant, and maybe so. I did what I had to do to survive and prosper, as did plenty of black people back then. But even when I was young, I had formed a whole outlook on life, and it didn't include any self-hatred. I knew who and what I was. I also knew discrimination happens. It was all around me. Still, think about this: Nobody has equal opportunity, including poor white folks.

Washington was a southern, segregated city in the 1950s, and those elected to the Senate at that time, no matter where they were from, thought they were entitled to the best that this country had to offer in the way of privileges. The luxurious Senate bath was a privilege, as was the barbershop. There was no charge for any of the services provided in either. In fact, senators at that time rarely had to pay for anything. They could send flowers for free to anyone for any occasion—girlfriends, wives, or both—just by picking up the phone and ordering some from the hothouse in southeast D.C., just off Howard Road.

They never had to pay for the food they ordered from the Senate restaurant, and could bring any friends to the place for lunch for free. Everything was on the government or the taxpayer.

Other kinds of services were free, too, back then, thanks to the biggest Senate perk of all at that time—us! The services of the capable downstairs staff were not restricted to the Senate but carried over to the outside. When the Senate was not in session and even sometimes when it was, the downstairs employees were sent to senators' homes, to fulfill any request required of them. If the senator had grown children who needed chores done, they were dispatched to the grown children's homes, where they were expected to do housework, babysitting, gardening, or whatever it was that the senator's family needed. Some served as bartenders and maids in senator's homes for parties. Yes, we were servants much of the time, but we took pride in our work.

On many occasions, George Smith, the Senate Wagon Master, went to the houses of the politicians and set up for the parties. Then a truck was assigned to pick up those downstairs employees who did not have transportation. The staff cleaned the house so it was spotless before the party, and then tidied up afterward.

Senate wives who were redecorating their homes would call upon the downstairs women at the Capitol to help. For example, Mrs. Wilhelmenia Simms, a black woman who made wonderful draperies, was in great demand among the spouses of the lawmakers, and kept herself busy during all of the seasons of the year. The Queen girls, Estelle, Bernice, and Edna, who were skilled at ironing, were frequently pulled from the Capitol halls to wash and iron clothes for a senator's wife. When overnight guests were expected, Senate employees were called upon to prepare the house, wash the bed linens, and change the beds. If the guest had children, one of the Capitol ladies would be sent over to the house to help the maid take care of them.

Fortunately, I was used mostly as a chauffeur. I drove senators' children and grandchildren to school and picked them up if their regular pick-up person was off. I took wives downtown to go shopping and waited for them patiently at the curb outside the store where D.C. policemen allowed me to stay in "no parking" zones because I was waiting for the wife of a senator. On my travels, I got to see a lot of Virginia and Maryland, and learned to handle a bus while driving Senate wives and others down to the Apple Blossom Festival in northern Virginia every year at the request of Virginia senator Harry Byrd. My trips also included driving Senate wives to the Crab Festival in Annapolis, Maryland. I was a jack-of-all-trades, however. If I was called on extra duty, I also stripped floors, cleaned garages, and cut the grass. In fact, some senators who lived on farms had downstairs staff out there doing farm work, but since everyone knew how I felt about working on a farm, I was never asked to do it.

We would work Saturdays, Sundays, and even some holidays. Although some senators tipped us or fed us with leftover food for our efforts, we received no salary for performing their house chores. Not a thin dime.

On the other hand, the senators were not the only ones who had "perks." The Senate was not in session from July through January, and if we were not needed by a senator we got most of that time off. Having six months off with pay every year was a big perk.

And there were other things. Being able to be sick and know that you did not have to worry about your paycheck was a great perk. Most blacks during that time did not have sick leave or maternity leave. Even the blacks who had janitors' jobs in other government agencies did not get paid when they did not work. Our benefits included free hospitalization for ourselves, and for our families as well, and full retirement security.

Most of the black people from South Carolina worked twenty-five to thirty years for local businesses and had only a small Social Security check to depend on for retirement, if that. They put in long years at bottling plants, bakeries, hospitals, oil companies, restaurants, and cafeterias in the area. Some companies did not even pay into Social Security.

When blacks retired from the Capitol, they got pensions. Most got pensions plus Social Security, because when you had that time off you sometimes worked in jobs where you were putting money into Social Security. Many of those guys were considered "well-to-do" after retirement, since they got a pension and Social Security. At a time when there were very few economic opportunities available for us, especially in a segregated city like Washington, we "downstairs employees" at the Capitol were acutely aware that our place of employment offered us more than we could get elsewhere in town, and we worked hard and with pride to do the best we could.

IN THE LATE 1950s, national newspapers and magazines were full of pictures of Rosa Parks sitting on a city bus, little Emmett Till's mother crying with a photo of her dead son killed by the Klan in Mississippi, and a young, short black man with a booming voice promising a bus boycott in Montgomery, Alabama, against prejudice. We on the Capitol staff watched as Reverend King fashioned a national campaign for equal rights in that segregated southern city but at first none of us southern black guys took him seriously. Even when King had his home bombed back then, we didn't think much of his chances of succeeding.

"Y'all heard about that preacher guy, Martin Luther King?" Jack asked us.

"I say he's a newcomer, that's all," someone replied.

"Me, too," another said. "Thurgood Marshall's been fightin' the good fight all these years, and now he comes along. Some say he's trying to steal the man's thunder."

Other guys spoke up. "Think about it, walkin' up and down streets. What good's *that* gonna do?"

"I've been walking up and down streets all my life." Jack laughed. "Hasn't changed nothing!"

We all laughed at his joke.

Furthermore, *The Baltimore Afro American* newspaper started playing up a feud between Thurgood Marshall, then the chief lawyer for the NAACP, and Martin Luther King, the new voice of the civil rights movement. The newspaper said King and Roy Wilkins, the new leader of the NAACP, believed in taking to the streets in protest, whereas Marshall believed the way to racial equality was through the courts and the legal system. We in the locker room were all on Marshall's side. We did not know a thing about Martin Luther King, Jr. or Roy Wilkins or freedom rides or protest marches in the South, and most of us did not think they would accomplish anything. History has obviously proven us wrong!

LIBERAL SENATORS HAD BEEN trying since the military services were integrated early in the 1950s to get a civil rights bill through Congress that would open housing, voting rights, restaurants, and public transportation to blacks. As the years went on, the bill got weaker and southern senators, who had opposed the measure before, became less vocal. By 1957, the Civil Rights Act was watered down to a voting-rights measure with little in the way of enforcement provisions, and the southern senators who had threatened to filibuster against the bill backed off. All except for one, that is.

Strom Thurmond was determined to support segregation by setting a new record—pulling off the longest filibuster. We downstairs guys found out about it when one of Thurmond's aides came down and asked Skeeter Johnson to get one of his handymen to make the senator a bag.

A bag? What kind of bag?

Well, a kind of special bag. See, the whole point was, Senator Thurmond wanted to filibuster for a record-breaking amount of time, and in order to talk and talk, the Senator would need to lubricate his vocal cords by drinking water, and that water had to go someplace. Since Senator Thurmond couldn't leave the chamber without ending the filibuster, he needed something that would prevent him from ever having to worry about heading for a urinal.

Our jaws dropped as one by one we realized what kind of bag Skeeter, the Secretary of the Senate, was being asked to have one of his employees put together.

Some might call it a fancy type of catheter. We all called it "THURMOND'S PEE BAG!"

It ended up being a rubber bag attached to the senator and taped to hang discreetly down his leg, so it wouldn't show. It ended in a clip that could be opened at the far end and then shut tightly once again.

On the day of the filibuster, the newspapers all reported that Senator Thurmond was bringing with him to the Senate floor huge amounts of reading materials, lozenges, and water in order to keep his filibuster going as long as he could, but *we* knew what the senator's real secret weapon was.

And we wanted nothing to do with it. This is one time we downstairs guys were *glad* we were not allowed on the Senate floor when it was in session, because Senator Thurmond needed an accomplice in order to pull off the pee-bag caper. During the filibuster, when he wanted to get rid of the urine, Thurmond walked over to a certain desk on the Senate floor, talking all the time. An aide would crawl on the floor under the desk, unhook the clip, and let the urine pour out into a jar. He would then reattach the clip, crawl out of the chamber with the jar, and take off to empty and clean it. None of this was seen by the public, because the aide was crawling on his knees and hidden by the desk.

Scroggins and Montgomery, our fellow downstairs employees, were stationed around the chamber door. When they saw the aide leaving with the urine jar hidden in a paper bag, they called down to the rest of us, and we would all disappear immediately. *No way* were we going to help empty and clean out that jar!

Without us around for support, Thurmond's aide had to do the messy work himself and do it quickly, because he had to get back to the Senate floor as fast as he could. Thurmond wanted to see him there at all times so he didn't have to worry about the bag overflowing.

All this was for a filibuster that accomplished nothing, since as soon as Thurmond finished speaking, the Senate passed the bill.

Man, I think we laughed for the entire twenty-four hours and eighteen minutes that Thurmond filibustered!

"They knew there was a jar, but didn't realize there was a pee bag," Jack told me afterward, in between gales of laughter. "They think he peed into the jar under the desk directly."

"Who thinks that?"

"Reporters!" Jack howled. "Reporters been calling Skeeter all day wanting to know who had to clean the pee off the floor when Thurmond missed!" He shook his head. "They assume some black guy had to mop it up." He leaned closer, his eyes sparkling. "They wanted to *interview* the guy!"

I laughed along with him. "What did Skeeter say?"

"Skeeter wanted *no* part of this. Skeeter cursed out the newspapers and hung up on them. He told us not to talk to anyone about helping to fix the bag."

During the historic filibuster, the senators stayed in the Senate all night, and the next day my picture was in the *Times Herald,* setting up cots for the sleepover. There was also a long article about those twenty-four hours and eighteen minutes of chatter against the civil rights provision. Reading the article made the filibuster a good deal less funny for me. Some of the things Thurmond had said about blacks really made my skin crawl. How could this man who had gone out of his way to be so kind and thoughtful to me and my family in South Carolina say such hateful things?

Again, I was struck by the dichotomy between what a politician said and did politically and what he said and did personally. No one was kinder to me than the "archsegregationist" Senator Strom Thurmond, who carried a lot of weight in the Senate and really looked out for me. Thurmond often invited me to have lunch with him in the Senate dining room. When schoolchildren or constituents came to Washington to meet with him, he would ask me to join them and sit and talk with them about South Carolina. "Listen, you let me know if you're not treated right," he said. "We South Carolina boys must stick together." Nobody messed with Thurmond, and, as a result, nobody messed with me.

Senator Olin Johnston, also from South Carolina, was also a good friend who went out of his way to introduce me to his family and friends when they came to visit.

I was never mistreated and I never got into trouble, so I never had to ask for help. Sometimes if you were black and got into trouble, you needed help from a benefactor. I knew a few downstairs employees who called their senator from jail to have him send an assistant to bail them out.

Blacks could not take out loans from the credit union on their own at that time. This did not bother me, because I still closely followed Senator Maybank's teachings, always keeping my bills paid and money in my pocket. But when others confronted serious money problems, they had few options. One of my friends got so far behind in his bills that people were calling the job and telling his supervisor that they were going to take his house. He worked for a senator, who sent a staff member to the credit union with the guy and took money out on the politician's signature.

I was then asked to accompany my friend to each bill collector, pay off his debts, and bring back the receipts to the senator.

Ever enterprising, I decided to drive a cab to earn a little extra money on weekends and evenings when I wasn't working at the Capitol. D.C. taxicabs are unlike any others. You buy a cab, take the test, and you are in business for yourself. You can work as many hours or as few as you want. It was the money that first enticed me. I was amazed by how much money in cold cash I could make right there and then—on the spot—rather than having to wait two weeks for it to come in a paycheck.

Gradually, however, I came to love the social part. D.C. was a less dangerous city back then, and it was an adventure for me to pick up a stranger on the corner and get him where he had to go. Every person was different, with a different story. For some reason, most people seemed to feel comfortable sharing their problems with a cab driver they would probably never see again. Sometimes I helped out with advice, and sometimes I just listened. I learned a lot, both good and bad, from mothers who were having problems with their children or men having troubles with their wives and girlfriends. I liked my role as "Ann Landers."

Every cab driver has what we call his "beat." Guys looking for runs to the airport, for example, can spot people standing on the corner with luggage from a mile away. Others hang around hotels because they think they get better tips that way.

It will come as no surprise to you that my "beat" was Union Station and the Capitol grounds. What I liked most was fooling people. I would pick up a Senate aide or some senator and he would look at me and say, "You look familiar."

"Well, I'm from South Carolina," I'd tell him, even though I knew he'd seen me in the halls of the Senate. "Are you from South Carolina?"

Then we would get into a conversation about politics and—again—because people feel comfortable sharing things with a cab driver they think they will never see again, I would almost always learn something I had not known.

"You know a lot about politics," the Senate aide would say as he got out of the car.

" I like to read the newspapers," I'd say.

"Well, keep it up and you'll go far some day!"

When the Senate was out of session, I often earned some extra money working for Strom Thurmond at his house out in Bethesda. I always thought of those as two-part exercise days. First, I did the heavy work he needed done while he relaxed, and then he invited me to talk with him on his back porch, where he would do his bodybuilding exercises as I relaxed. The man was a physical fitness nut way ahead of the craze. He was a good thirty years older than I was, but just as thin and infinitely more agile.

"This exercise is for Myrtle Beach next week," he told me one afternoon as he did his sit-ups. "For a ladies' man like me, there's nothing better than lookin' at all those beauties go by in their swimming suits on Myrtle Beach."

"You don't have to be in shape to look at girls," I pointed out, laughing.

"Well, there's always the hope they'll look back! Girls like a man who's physically fit." He paused for a moment, catching his breath, and nodded at the dumbbells he had hanging on the wall. "Pick up one, Bertie," he urged. "Build up your muscles."

I stared at the weights. "They look kinda like the hams and bacon they used to hang out to dry back home," I said.

"Gotta give up some of that southern food," he cautioned. "It's good but it ain't good for you." He crouched forward, his elbows down, his knees bent, and I groaned, knowing from experience what was coming next. Sure enough, next thing I knew, the senator from South Carolina was standing on his head.

"C'mon Bertie," he said, "Try it. Great for balance."

I looked at him, deadpan. "Man, I've been stripping and sanding your floors all day. If you think I'm going to stand on my head for exercise, you're crazy!"

We both got a laugh out of that.

EVEN THOUGH I'D PASSED the cab exam, there were still addresses in the city I didn't know how to get to. I confided my worries to Ivory Oliver and Lee Johnson, buddies from South Carolina who were experienced cab drivers. Older and wiser, they had persuaded me to take the exam and get a cab in the first place. "I pick up these diplomats and people from out of town, and they give me an address," I complained, "and sometimes I have to *pretend* I know where it is."

Ivory, who knew his way around, shook his head. "You know the area, Bertie!"

"Not thoroughly," I said. "A whole lot of time I get them to where they're going by accident! It's hit-and-miss."

"Accident is good enough, just as long as you get them there." Lee laughed. "Man, get that sad look off your face. Act like you know what you're doing. Remember, these people don't know where they're going either. If you smile and go around and around and around the corner until you find it, they won't know that you don't know. They don't live here."

I acted on those suggestions one day when I picked up three Asian diplomats in front of the Capitol. They wanted to go to the Japanese Embassy on Massachusetts Avenue. Well, I knew where Massachusetts was, but it was dark, too dark to be able to read the name of the Embassy on the buildings and my passengers did not have an address.

I did not know where in the heck I was going. I rode up and down Massachusetts for almost an hour. In fact, I think I passed that embassy six times, going around and around in a circle. My passengers, who could not speak much English, seemed very happy in my backseat as they kept looking out the window and saying, "Beautiful Washington, beautiful Washington!" We drove up one side of Massachusetts and down the other. They did not even seem to notice that we were stuck on the same street. Each time we got to a traffic light, I would take out my map as if I knew where we were, and, with my flashlight, try to find the address of the Japanese Embassy.

Finally, I looked up and saw a lot of Asian ladies and men all dressed up getting out of a limousine in the driveway of one of those embassies. I wisely drove right into that driveway as if I knew where I was going. My passengers in the backseat began talking very fast and laughing and pointing at the people outside the car. Sure enough, they *recognized* some of them. When they got out, they began bowing and thanking me and saying: "Thank you! Beautiful Washington, beautiful Washington!" Since they gave me a really big tip, I assumed they did not know that we'd passed the place six times. Lucky for me.

I heaved a sigh of relief, put my "off duty" sign in the window and headed for home. I could not wait to tell Ivory and Lee the next day.

When I got to the locker room the following day, the three of us laughed about that embassy episode for a long time. Joking, we would bow to each other, hold our hands out and say: "Beautiful Washington, beautiful tip!"

IN 1961, I was called back to active duty in the Air National Guard during the Berlin Crisis and then again in 1962 during the Cuban Missile Crisis. I was stationed at Andrews Air Force Base the whole time. Since I was a sergeant and living within fifty miles of the base, I was permitted to live at home, which I loved, and because I worked as a supervisor in food service, I was on a schedule where I worked two full days and then was off for three full days. On the off days, we did not have to be around the base, so I naturally gravitated to the only real home I'd ever had—the United States Capitol. I was getting paid by the Air Force and had no reason to go to the Capitol, other than to be in the company of my "family." In the time I spent there, I would play cards with the guys, help some of the older men get their work done, work in the library, and do anything anyone wanted me to do. This was my pleasure. I just loved being there.

Every so often we were sent from Andrews to Savannah, Georgia, for a week of training, and there I got to spend time with my blood relatives. My cousins Gladys and Joe Bazemore, who lived in Savannah, frequently invited me and my friends from the base for dinner, good old southern cooking.

At those dinners, I learned a lot about my family's history from Gladys and her aunt Kate, who told me stories I'd never heard before about my father's background. Summerton was only two hours away from Savannah, and gradually my siblings began coming down to the Bazemores' to visit me. My sisters Charlotte and Annie drove down for dinner every so often. My sister Dot was away at college at the time. My brother Larry was in the service and my sister Wilhelmenia was living in Washington, D.C., with her husband, Bobby Bennett.

When I finally got off active duty and returned to the Capitol in 1963, Mr. Hubner, the librarian, took me to see Skeeter Johnson.

"Bertie just got back from the Air Force and he needs a job," Hubner said. "We gave his job to Montgomery's boy while he was gone. We got to get him back on the payroll."

"Air Force," Skeeter said excitedly. "You were in the *Air Force, Bertie?*"

I nodded.

"Well, what do you know? My son is going into the Air Force next week and I want you to talk to him." To my surprise, he picked up the phone, called his son, and told him to come to the Capitol right away. "I want you to talk to someone who just came back from the Air Force," he said.

As I sat there waiting for Skeeter's son, I couldn't help wondering what had happened to the job discussion we were supposed to have and why he wanted *me* to talk to his son. Surely there was no shortage of Air Force veterans from Mississippi to talk to.

When his son arrived, Skeeter introduced us, called up the cafeteria, and told them to make lunch for the two of us. "Now, Bertie," Skeeter said, ushering us out the door, "you need to tell him what to do and what not to do when he gets in there next week."

It was only at lunch that I realized what was happening. We got along very well, but the son's questions were not about what life was like in the Air Force. Instead he wanted my advice about how to talk to blacks and how to get along with blacks. Skeeter Johnson, a white man from Mississippi, wanted his son to know how to get along with black people, now that the Air Force was desegregated. He knew that getting along with black enlisted men would make his time in the service go better.

The world was certainly changing!

When we returned from lunch, Skeeter and I had our talk.

"Bertie, you've got a very good employment record. I can get you a job at the Pentagon."

"No," I quickly replied.

"Well, then, how about the Printing Office?" He wanted to get me a better job, or at least one he thought was better. But I wanted to stay with the guys, my "family."

"No. I want to stay at the Capitol."

"Now, listen, Bertie, at these other jobs, you'd start at a much higher salary—"

"No." I didn't want to change jobs.

"And you could move up quickly. Someone who works as hard as . . ."

"NO!"

"Okay." He sighed. "You can work for me then." He finally gave up.

I'm not a person who loves change. I knew the Capitol and the guys there, so I became a messenger. Also, I knew the kind of man and boss that Skeeter would be.

IN 1963, Reverend Martin Luther King was planning on coming to Washington with a huge number of blacks to demonstrate for civil rights, and the Kennedy White House was not happy about it. That was the word in the locker room.

As usual, Jack gave us the lowdown. "King's at the White House right now, talking to the President 'n' Bobby," he said. "That's why things are so tight over there."

Another one of the guys pointed something out to us. "Won't even let messengers in! They told us to leave the packages outside and leave the grounds right away!"

"Kennedy don't want no march!" someone said.

"Kennedy gonna stop that march!" another added.

As it turned out, President Kennedy apparently couldn't stop the March on Washington, so he put in a few measures to keep the peace if matters got out of hand. Fearful a demonstration in Washington, D.C., might become violent like the ones in the South that were getting top news headlines, he called out the National Guard to ensure that everything would not boil over.

In other words, he called out me.

This time I reported to Andrews Air Force Base, where my Air National Guard group was assigned to help guard the Capitol from what was expected to be a potentially violent group of demonstrators heading toward the city for the 1963 March on Washington for Jobs and Freedom.

It was a very hot August in a year that had been characterized by civil rights demonstrations in the South and across the country. There were newspaper photos and television footage of police turning attack dogs and fire hoses against protestors in Birmingham, Alabama. Reverend Martin Luther King was arrested, along with several protestors, and wrote his now-famous "Letter from a Birmingham Jail" advocating civil disobedience against unjust laws.

The March on Washington was sponsored by five different civil rights groups, each of which had a slightly different approach to civil rights, and was opposed by extremists on both sides of the issue, such as white-supremacist groups like the Ku Klux Klan and Civil Rights radicals, like Malcolm X, who advocated stronger action.

We now know, of course, that the 1963 March on Washington turned out to be a historic turning point in the struggle to get national Civil Rights laws passed. It was the largest demonstration the nation's capital had ever experienced, and a very peaceful one, but it was the first of its kind and in the days leading up to it some people were anticipating riots in the streets of Washington.

Guarding the Capitol turned out to be extremely easy, since all the action was happening at the Lincoln Memorial, at the other end of the Mall, and no demonstrators even showed up at the Capitol. I stayed on my post for a while but then took most of the guys in my squad inside the Capitol so we could watch the speeches on television.

By the time Reverend King spoke, everyone came inside, even the Capitol Police, and the television sets were on in every available office. People also crowded around in halls and doorways to listen to radios. Meanwhile, police, National Guardsmen, and Capitol employees, both white and black, all stood around together watching televisions, with no one making a sound, just listening intently. The minister gave a glorious speech of love, brotherhood, and healing that nobody will ever forget.

Some people had never heard Reverend King address a crowd before. Also, I think a lot of the white people had never heard a black person speak so articulately before.

When Dr. King began chanting "Free at Last" in his melodic voice, cheers poured out of all the offices on the floor. Some clapped and others wept. More than 250,000 Americans gathered on the steps of the Lincoln Memorial and the Mall without incident, after being led in the march by the black leaders A. Philip Randolph and Bayard Rustin. But they were waiting to hear the fiery southern reverend stir the folks, and this he did. I felt proud, so very proud.

The guys in the locker room were not wild about the Kennedys because the leading black newspapers told us our hero, Thurgood Marshall, said he was not wild about President Kennedy or his younger brother. He thought they could do more for people of color, and we found facts to support that argument. Many of the guys pointed out that when most senators had many blacks in clerical positions in their offices in the late 1950s, Senator John F. Kennedy did not. When Kennedy became president, he had few blacks on his office staff, and Attorney General Bobby Kennedy had few on his staff at the Justice Department.

And so the conversation in the locker room in the aftermath of the Kennedy assassination was dramatically different from what was being said in the rest of the country. We were strong supporters of Lyndon Johnson. We couldn't stop talking about our new president, a man who stood up for blacks, as evidenced by a classic LBJ anecdote we had all heard and told repeatedly in the course of twenty-four hours after the assassination in Dallas.

One of our fellow Capitol staff members, Norman Edwards, and his wife had worked for the Johnsons in both Texas and Washington for decades. Norman had served as the Johnsons' driver throughout LBJ's political career and continued in that post when Johnson became vice president.

After President Kennedy's assassination, Johnson was sworn in as president on the plane heading back to Washington. When the plane landed at Andrews Air Force Base, Norman was there to pick him up, as he always was.

An exhausted Johnson got off the plane, walked toward his car and said, "Come on, Norman. Let's go home." As he started to get in, a Secret Service Agent stopped him.

"No, Mr. President, he can't drive you," the agent said.

"What are you talking about?" Johnson growled, "This man has been driving me for years!"

"You are the President of the United States," the Secret Service Agent replied firmly, "And you must have a member of the Secret Service drive you from now on."

"Goddamnit, this man's driving me," Johnson raged. "Then go ahead—make him a member of the Secret Service right now. I don't need a new driver."

After they put in a call to their superiors, the agents asked Norman to raise his hand, and they temporarily made him a Secret Service agent. It was Norman who drove Johnson home that night.

He remained the driver for President Johnson because the powerful man from Texas made sure he got the Secret Service training he needed to do so. With that training, he became one of the first black Secret Service members to protect the president.

That story always tickled the downstairs guys. "Goddamnit!" one guy in the locker room shouted in a mock Texas drawl, laughing.

"Make him Secret Service!" another one answered in that familiar cowboy accent.

The downstairs guys all loved Lyndon Johnson, because he was larger than life, and he stood up for his employees. I saw quite a bit of President Johnson in my new messenger job, because, in addition to delivering things around the Capitol, it was my responsibility to take bills and whatever else was in those large envelopes to the White House.

Anyone familiar with the post-9/11 security measures in Washington, especially around the White House, would be shocked to see the way things were back in the 1960s. Those were the days when you could walk in and out of the White House with nothing more than a Senate pass. I used to drive the Secretary of the Senate's car right up to the door, and nobody even asked to see my pass, because they all recognized me. I entered the side door and walked right over to the desk outside of President Johnson's Oval Office. The guards were all Marines, and I just waved the envelope at them and kept walking.

Johnson remembered me from the Senate barbershop, and sometimes when he was not busy he would invite me into his office to chat. We talked about the good old days after the war or the politicians back in those times. We had many a good laugh. Also, he told a rough joke or two. Sometimes he walked in his long strides out to the secretary's desk to say hello and invite me to go down to the kitchen and get some lunch. They had a well-stocked kitchen in the basement of the White House that was just for employees, with some very good food. It was all so relaxed. Times have changed dramatically.

One day, something happened that would change my life. I was driving my cab early one evening from a run out in the northeast when I saw an attractive woman leaning against an ugly Army-green colored car hailing a cab at 49th and Jay Streets. She was wearing a short fur jacket and a black skirt that revealed nice-looking legs. She had a bundle of stuff in her arms, another bundle on the trunk of the car, and a briefcase on the sidewalk by the car's back wheel.

I stopped.

She hopped in, filling my backseat with papers and leather bundles. She gave me the address of a church in the northwest section of the city. "I'm so glad you stopped," she said. "My car broke down, and I have to get there on time."

When I looked back, I saw the sheer beauty of her face—her bright eyes, dimples, and a pretty smile. "What's all that?" I asked, nodding at the mess in my backseat.

"It's my music," she said. "I am a singer."

"What kind of singing goes on in a Baptist church on a weeknight?"

She tried to gather the papers in a neat pile. "Oh, it's a rehearsal. Baptist churches have a holy week of music the week before Easter. Their choirs do the choral work, and we're hired to sing the solos."

"Who is 'we'?" I asked, glancing at her.

"We are a group of voice majors who graduated with me from Howard's Music School," she said, looking through the papers.

I nodded.

"See?" she said and handed me one of the fliers. "This is the schedule of all the performances we're going to do."

I glanced at the paper and put it down on the seat next to me. "Is that what you do for a living?"

"No," she said. "For extra money. I have a different job full-time." She leaned forward. "Listen, could we stop first at the Main Post Office on North Capitol? I've got a whole bunch of stuff I have to mail, and I need to buy stamps first."

"Ah, you're one of those," I joked. "Gonna run off at the post office without paying me!"

She smiled again, an even friendlier one this time. "Look, I'll leave all my music here in the cab with you. Believe me, it's more valuable than I am. Isn't that good enough assurance that I'll return?"

"Nope." It was getting dark and I wanted to get a better look at her. "I'll come into the post office with you, just to be sure." I pulled to the curb and parked. I helped her out of the cab.

In the post office, there were two or three people ahead of her in line. I liked the way she walked in high heels. Her legs were shapely, easy on the eyes.

I held the door open for her when we got back to the cab. "So what are you singing for the Baptists?"

Her voice was like a group of lyrical notes, which I really liked. " 'The Seven Last Words.' I'm a lyric soprano, so I do the soprano solo."

"Impressive," I said, wondering what "The Seven Last Words" was. I wondered if she could really sing, hold a tune. Truthfully, I was tone-deaf but I knew good music when I heard it.

"Thank you so much," she said as she paid me when we got to the church. She smiled, got out, and ran off.

I watched her. Then I looked down at the schedule she'd left in my front seat. I picked it up and circled the time and place of the first concert on Monday. I smiled and pinned the schedule to my sun visor. I wanted to see her again. And I liked music.

This turned out to be a very different sort of music. I knew jazz and church music, but I did not know anything about the kind of singing I heard when I attended that first concert. It was like being in an opera house. She put her head back, closed her eyes, and sounds came out that I had never heard before. I was so shocked and so moved by her voice. When she finished her first solo, I burst into applause. I did not know you were not supposed to clap. Fortunately, I was not the only one in the church who did not know you were not supposed to clap.

I went up to her after that performance. "Remember me?" I asked, and then when she did not seem to remember added, "I'm the cab driver who brought you here to the rehearsal."

"Oh, yes, of course! Thank you for coming!" She was genuinely pleased.

"Is your car working?" I asked her, hoping it wasn't. "Do you need a ride?"

"No." She laughed. "My car is working fine . . . but thank you." She turned to talk to someone else.

On Tuesday, after the second concert, I approached her again. "Do you remember me now?" I asked.

She did a double take. "Do you mean we were *so* good you wanted to hear us two days in a row?"

I grinned at her. "Do you need a ride?"

"No." She laughed, "My car is working fine!" But there was something about the way she looked at me that told me she was interested, too. And then, of course, there were those dimples.

I tried the same tactic on Wednesday. I was determined to let her know I was not going to give up. This time she recognized me, and so did her fellow singers, but she still did not need a ride.

On Thursday, the day of the last concert, I came early, and I saw her when she drove up in her car and parked, but I made sure that she did not see me, not that she would have noticed. She seemed to be always rushing, always in a hurry.

After she went into the church, I decided to sit in the car and listen to the concert from the outside. As the concert went on, I did some serious questioning. Sure I liked this woman. I liked the way she looked, the way she behaved, the way she sang. But now, let's get serious. For all I knew, she could have had a boyfriend, or even be *married* for that matter. I had watched her very carefully and, after turning down my offer of a ride each time, she had never left with anyone else. So maybe there was nobody in her life.

I came up with two other possibilities. One was a painful prospect:

"Maybe she just does not like me." The other was just as frightening: "Maybe she has to rush home to a husband and six or seven kids!" I sat there with my fingers crossed, hoping neither was true. I also hoped that maybe—just maybe—the strategy of staying outside would work, that she would be disappointed when she did not see me sitting there at the concert and say "yes" this time when I asked her if she needed a ride.

And if she said no, I would ask her to dinner.

The concert ended. I watched her carefully. She was socializing, but I was certain she was looking around for someone. Finally, she gathered her stuff together, said good-bye to her group, and walked out.

"Do you need a ride?" I asked, coming up behind her.

She smiled. Pretty. Dimples. "I sure do!" she said, "My car is broken and I was going to catch a cab."

That statement gave me a lot of courage. I had, after all, seen her drive up and park a perfectly functioning car just before the start of the concert. "Well, here's a cab right here," I said, opening the front door this time, not the back door.

She got in. I took her music and choir robes from her, put them in the trunk, and climbed into the driver's seat. "Do you like seafood?" I asked her.

"I love seafood."

"I know a wonderful seafood restaurant, and you've got to be hungry after all that singing. Would you like to go have dinner with me?"

"Yes."

Pretty smile. Dimples. "What's your name?" I asked.

"Elaine."

Nothing in my lifetime did more to alter the racial landscape of this country than the 1964 Civil Rights Act, which banned discrimination in employment, housing, and public accommodations. While millions of blacks used the provisions of that law to alter their lives drastically in the years since its passage, I was the only one I know to have used its debate as a means of wooing a woman.

The Civil Rights Act completely preoccupied the Senate for fifty-seven working days, and everyone knew that the law, if passed, would mark a historic turning point for the country. Including the new beautiful woman in my life, Elaine.

Elaine was fascinated by the whole political process, the pros and cons of the entire debate in the Congress. She was very keen to listen to the debate. I got her a free parking space and a month-long pass, enabling her to go to the Senate Gallery anytime she wanted. Most tourists could only stay for an hour at a time, but since I knew all the tour guides, they let Elaine stay as long as she wanted. After a while, she even secured a special seat for herself in the corner.

Some of the hearings went late into the night. Two or three days a week, in June of 1964, Elaine left her job at The Center for Applied Linguistics and went to the Gallery, thrilled to be able to listen to "history in the making." I was thrilled that she was thrilled, because we were working so late those nights that there was no other way I would have been able to see her.

Some men bring women home to "meet the family." I guess this was my equivalent, because in so many ways the Senate was my home. I introduced Elaine to the many members of my Senate "family," and then, when I got off work, I took her to the Senate dining room for dinner. By that time, all my buddies were usually busy cleaning up, but Mr. Johnson and Mr. Dallis, looking splendid in their white jackets, found time nonetheless to serve me and my future wife leftovers at a beautifully appointed table that was covered with a white tablecloth and had fresh flowers in the middle.

Something Personal

SOMETIMES THINGS HAPPEN IN LIFE THAT YOU CANNOT EXPLAIN. Sometimes you feel at loose ends, like things are not going well and maybe won't go well at all. Sometimes women go in and out of your life, taking a little part of yourself. I don't like to talk much about myself and my personal life, especially with love and women. When Senator Maybank died in 1954, I was feeling low, out of sorts, and still in the service with the side job at the Capitol. I used to study guys who were so assured, confident, acting like they owned the world. I wasn't one of these guys. I was still shy in many ways. I was very young. It was probably the only period of my life where I temporarily lost my bearings, lost my way, and that was when my brother, Charlie, introduced me to a woman I thought I loved. We got married but we never lived together, for she was living in New York and I in D.C.

My first wife, who will remain nameless, respected my decision to maintain my Capitol job and the military assignment, yet she refused to join me—even after I worked extra hours to buy a house. On some weekends, I would go to New York to see her, and in the course of our wedlock, we became a family with four children: Gregory, Annetta, Charlene, and Wilbert. Eventually the conflicts grew as our love soured, until we ended our union without too much fanfare. I always paid child support for my children, but it was a sad thing that I could not spend as much time as I wanted with my flesh and blood. I tried to get all of us together with a home in the Washington area, but that failed.

My first wife could hardly be held responsible for the fact that she didn't want to relocate, however. I made some wrong choices and you do that when you're very young, as I was. I was never a ladies' man. Some of the older guys, like Willie, told me that when you're "wet behind the ears" you should keep your mouth shut and stay out of everyone's way. Mama said that as well. I was not a crybaby. When I was with the guys in the locker room, I never shared information about my relationship or the problems with my private life. It was none of their business.

The moment of awakening came about when I met Elaine, with her pretty stranded self, for I quickly began to make several changes and mature from almost every experience. For years, all I wanted was to move away from the farm, start working an honest job, buy my home, get married, start a family, and have a good life. But that was not to be. We all have to face a big crisis in our lives, yet for me it was about what you do to recover and straighten yourself out.

Courting Elaine opened a new world for me. She gave me an impression that she wanted to see more of me, that she was very interested. As a teacher, she could be probing, very smart and analytical. I never knew where our discussions would lead and that was all right with me. I had never met a woman like her.

One night, while sitting in my car Elaine asked me, "Bertie, so what do you think you have to offer a woman?" She asked the question with a straight face. Nobody ever asked me questions like this. Usually when you took out a woman, the talk was pretty light and breezy. However, I wanted Elaine to see me and know that I could be serious, looking within myself at the meaning of my life. I wanted her to know that I was a good man.

"I want to have a good life, do the right things, and make the right choices," I answered. "I watch what I do and say. I know the power of

April 1951
Official Army photograph after completing basic training. U.S. Army 100 1st Airborne Division, Camp Breckinridge, Kentucky. (*Bertie Bowman Collection*)

1951
Unsure of what was to come in my life, I smiled and posed for this picture in Seattle, Washington, at Fort Lewis Army Transport Base just before I was shipped out to Korea. (*Bertie Bowman Collection*)

Summer of 1952, South Korea
Joking around in front of the road grader before learning how to drive it. (*Bertie Bowman Collection*)

Winter 1952, South Korea
I was the company mail man. (32nd Group Engineer Construction Battalion, Company C.) (*Bertie Bowman Collection*)

Senate "All-Night Session," 1955
Bob Collins (janitorial supervisor) and I prepare the room for the planned all-night Senate session. Cots and pillows were brought in for the senators who were going to participate in the all-night sessions. (*U.S. Senate staff photographer*)

1966
Senator J. William Fulbright presents me with one of the first pins awarded to a U.S. Senate employee for Loyal Service. I cherish this pin and continue to wear it every day. "Bertie is never without his Service Pin," Senator Pell always said. (*U.S. Senate staff photographer*)

"We, the People." 1966
Formal picture of the Senate Foreign Relations Committee. (*Courtesy of the U.S. Capitol Historical Society*)

1971
Senator J. William Fulbright and Mrs. Betty Fulbright enjoy the Valentine's Day staff party at the Bowman home. (*LaUanah King-Cassell*)

President Jimmy Carter, 1976
Here I am with Senator Frank Church, welcoming President-Elect Jimmy Carter to the Foreign Relations Committee. Carter was the only president-elect to testify before the Committee. (*U.S. Senate staff photographer*)

The First Party, 1983

I had long complained about how under-appreciated and uncelebrated the Senate's "downstairs" workers were when they retired, so I finally did something about it and threw a retirement party for all downstairs employees who had retired, or were about to retire, after working decades in the Senate. The guest list was huge, and they came—some on walkers, some with canes, some in wheelchairs, some with medication, but they all came and had a great time. And we hoped, felt appreciated. (*Ronald C. Howard*)

The First Party, 1983

On the back porch of my home, five of my mentors took a picture with me to celebrate our friendship and the wonderful years we worked together. These guys nicknamed me "Young Blood" and deserve all of the credit for my success, especially "Jack." *From left to right:* Willie Young, custodian; Bill Gardner, first black printing clerk for the Senate; George Johnson, messenger; Theodore "Jack" Jackson, assistant to Mickey, my first boss and locker room "Boss Man"; George McIvory, custodian. (*Ronald C. Howard*)

October 1985
After the success of the first party, the retired downstairs employees wanted to have another one. So, two years later I did it again and fun was had by all. (*Ronald C. Howard*)

Out and About
While taking a break from my Saturday taxi cab job I stopped to chat with Mayor Marion Barry who was campaigning for his Ward 8 candidate. (*Elaine Bowman*)

Community Involvment
Receiving an award from D.C. Chief of Police Issac Fulwood and Community Service officer
Sue McGinnis for outstanding work with the Neighborhood Watch Program.
(*Elaine Bowman*)

The Limo Service
Me in our garage, washing our two limousines just before going out on a job. (*Elaine Bowman*)

Retirement 1990
Me and Elaine with Senator Sanford at my retirement party. (*U.S. Senate staff photographer*)

Good luck
It filled my heart when Senator Nancy Kassenbaum gave me a big hug and wished me "good luck" at my retirement party. (*U.S. Senate staff photographer*)

Three Southern Gentlemen, 2003
Me and Senators Helms and Thurmond. (*U.S. Senate staff photographer*)

In the Oval Office
After a wonderful day at the White House, President Clinton pauses to take a picture with me and Elaine. *(Official White House photograph/Bertie Bowman Collection)*

Helms and Albright
While I stood by his side, Senator Helms thanks Secretary Albright after a Foreign Relations Committee hearing. (*U.S. Senate staff photographer*)

Secretary Shultz
After a long day of testifying at a Senate Foreign Relations Committee hearing, Secretary George Shultz takes a break to chat with me about baseball. (*U.S. Senate staff photographer*)

Secretary Baker
Helping Secretary Jim Baker set up his props before his confirmation hearing. (*U.S. Senate staff photographer*)

"Just Doing My Job"
Checking the agenda with then Chairman Richard Lugar, as Senator Chuck Hagel looks on.
(*U.S. Senate staff photographer*)

"End of the Day Fun"
Senator Joe Biden always ends my day on a happy note. He is a very busy and serious chairman in sessions, but he is always pleasant and full of humor off the dais. (*U.S. Senate staff photographer*)

Secretary of State Condoleezza Rice
Dr. Rice and I talk about football, baseball, and music while she was waits to be called back to the witness table. (*Susan Oursler*)

70th Anniversary of the Senate Federal Credit Union, 2006
Senators Richard Lugar and Elizabeth Dole celebrate with me. (*U.S. Senate staff photographer*)

my own will. I know I must take responsibility for myself and my own life. I try to look at the lessons that life offers. Mama always said look before you leap. I was never a man to fuss and fight. I am a doer."

At the following dinners and events during our courtship, she asked many questions, examining me to my core. I was very honest with her. We talked about ourselves freely, our bad unions and our upcoming divorces. We ended up saying that we never wanted to get married again but our hearts started to overrule us.

"Do you like your men to be domesticated?" I joked as we walked under the cherry blossoms at the Mall.

"I only want the man to be a man," she replied, her dimples on show. "And be reliable and have a good heart. Be loving and responsible."

I could understand Elaine's stress on reliability. She had been hitched when she was very young and went against her family to team with her man. She was the mother of a young girl, LaUanah, whose father was her high school sweetheart before her early marriage.

"Do you believe a woman should work outside the home?" I asked her.

"Why not?" She was feisty, and I liked that.

"So you don't believe a man's dinner should be ready when he comes home?"

We both laughed a long time about that because she knew I was joking. We finally broke the ice on talking about marriage, a topic that we had avoided until now. She was bold about the subject and wanted me not to tell her what she expected to hear. She wanted the truth about me and my intentions.

"You know, there was a time when I was looking for a doctor, lawyer, or dentist, but now after what I went through with my marriage, I just want a good person," she said to me, looking straight in my eyes.

I nodded. I understood that, for I knew her story.

"The way I see it is that a good marriage is when you have a life that I respect, and I have a life that you respect, and we have a life together," I said.

She was still puzzled. "What does this mean?"

Before I answered her question, I asked, "Are we serious about this relationship?"

She smiled and said yes before I even finished the sentence.

"Well, if you are, we will be together for a long time and I won't have to explain what it means," I finally said. We met in 1964 but could not get married until 1969. At that time, you had to be separated for five years before a divorce was granted. It changed both of our lives, for the better.

After that day, I felt I needed someone to talk with "man to man" because I felt that I was really falling in love. Head over heels. So I called my best friend and Army buddy, Elmer Brown, who lived around the corner. We had much in common. Not only had Elmer and I been through the Army National Guard together, but both of us had been through bad marriages together. I told him how deeply I was beginning to feel about Elaine, and he surprised me by telling me about Johnnie, a wonderful woman who had just "knocked him off his feet." We laughed together at our chance encounters, our good luck with women, and had a manly talk about how the "love bug" had bitten both of us at the same time.

To this day, we are still the best of friends. He's like a brother. There is nothing we wouldn't do for each other.

I HAD TAKEN STEPS over the years to try to compensate for the education I'd missed by running away from home and school at such a young age. After taking evening courses while working during the day and finally getting my high school diploma from Washington's Armstrong Senior High School, I decided perhaps it was time to use the G.I. Bill and get a college degree. After all, colleges had night courses, too.

Oblivious to the fact that you were supposed to *get in* to college, I stopped by the admissions office at Howard University one day and told them I wanted to be a student there. I thought that was the way you got into college. They gave me an application to fill out, and I was shocked at how long it was, with countless pages and endless questions. I had my high school send my grades along to Howard, mailed in the application, and waited.

And waited and waited. When I'd heard nothing for a month, I went back to Howard, and they told me that I could not get into the school because my grades were not high enough. I was very disappointed but concluded that perhaps college was not for everyone.

"And what's happening with your college plans?" Senator Thurmond asked me one day when we were talking in his office.

That was a question that I wanted to avoid. "I applied to Howard, but they said my high school grades weren't high enough." I shrugged.

His eyes narrowed. "What do you mean?"

I explained the rejection of my application in greater detail.

The next thing I knew he was on the phone. "This is Senator Strom Thurmond, calling for Bill Roberts." Thurmond leaned back in his office chair and waited with a serious look on his face. "Bill? Senator Thurmond here. Now, I have this fine young man from my home state, who just told me that you won't let him in that school up there. I can't imagine what is going on. I mean, as we both know, most of the money you get to run that school comes from the federal government . . ."

And so it went on in this manner for several minutes as my eyes roamed over the pictures hanging on the walls, and I wondered if this was such a great idea. I only heard one side of the conversation, but it was so forceful and intense that there were times I questioned whether anyone was on the other end.

"Thank you very much," the senator said before hanging up.

After a few minutes, he looked at me with that withering stare that made his fellow lawmakers tremble. "Bertie, now you go right back up to Howard and ask to see William Roberts in the Office of Administration," he instructed. "He should have some good news for you."

I will never forget how everyone up at Howard treated me when I walked into the office. They were bowing and scraping. I did not have to fill out any forms. I did not even have to pay for that first semester. They just told me that I would be taking a political science class to see how I felt about the university and told me where and when to report.

I was going to be a student at Howard University! I told everybody. I went out and bought a briefcase and notebooks. I was awed by the power conveyed by those three little words: "Senator Strom Thurmond."

The three words turned out to be equally powerful but overwhelmingly negative when, at the beginning of my first class, the professor introduced me to the other students, all of whom were black, as "a friend of Senator Strom Thurmond."

I smiled, but I was the only one in the room who did. It didn't take long for me to realize that the students were all wondering "*How* could you be *his* friend?" And the professor did not like that he'd had to accept a student in his class who had not qualified on his own, simply because of a phone call from the powerful senator from the state of South Carolina. Well, I did not do well, because I was not prepared for higher education with my weak academic skills. I think I knew this beforehand.

College, I decided, was perhaps not for everyone.

In time, Skeeter Johnson retired and a new face replaced him. Emory Frazier became Secretary of the Senate. One day in 1966, Frazier called me into his office. He told me he'd just gotten off the phone with Carl Marcy, the Chief of Staff of the Foreign Relations Committee. "Senator Fulbright wants you to work for him," Frazier announced, "as his chauffeur and as a staff member of the committee."

I could not believe it. I enjoyed working in the library, but I liked driving better. I still remembered the allure of the black chauffeurs parked and chatting back home. Now, I was going to be hired as the one and only driver for the most important senator in the Senate, William Fulbright, Chairman of the Senate Foreign Relations Committee! As excited as a young boy, I ran up to the empty committee room, just to look around.

As I stood there, looking around, a nice well-dressed black lady tapped me on the shoulder. "Hi, Bertie. I'm Thomasina Smith," she said. "Welcome to the Foreign Relations Committee."

Mrs. Smith was no stranger to me. She had supervised the downstairs guys many times when we were assigned committee duty. She helped me to learn my way around the rules and traditions of the "upstairs" world, and her husband, a prominent D.C. lawyer, gave me free legal advice whenever I needed it.

Change had come to the Congress, and several black staff members were getting a chance to move up. This was part of a changing racial demographic that enabled many downstairs guys to get promotions into better assignments upstairs during the 1960s. We all knew the names: Leon DeVille moved to the Appropriations Committee; Bruce Harris to the Atomic Energy Committee; Oscar Quarles and Bennie Hoban to the Documents Room; George McLean and Herman Scott to the Library; and George Smith became the Wagon Master. I was not the first to move up. I was part of a trend.

It was a trend bucked by many of the older downstairs employees. People like Jack, Mickey, and many of my former mentors wanted to stay where they were, in familiar positions, because they had done the same job for years and were comfortable with that. They were not all that thrilled with the idea of change, but some of us youngbloods were up for the challenge.

The next day, I sat down with Senator Fulbright to discuss the job. I would be "assistant to the committee's chief clerk," who was Buddy Kindrick at the time. It was an invented job. Kindrick did not have any assistant before I got there. Fulbright was just trying to get a good, reliable, honest driver for him and his wife. The title "assistant to the clerk" sounded better than a lesser one of Chauffeur/Committee clerical assistant/boy Friday. At that time, if a senator wanted someone to work for him, he would just grab him and then invent a job for him.

Senator Fulbright explained to me that he was making me a Committee employee to guarantee me a measure of job security. If I worked strictly for him, the old rules said that I could be fired if either he lost a re-election campaign or the Republicans took over the Senate. But this way, with a bipartisan committee job I would be relatively safe, no matter what happened. I was very grateful, knowing all too well how quickly staff members lost their jobs when their senator lost an election.

Since I was an employee of the Committee, I had to take an oath. I got all dressed up in a new suit and raised my hand and repeated the words as Senator Fulbright recited them aloud in front of a group of other staff members. When I got to the "so help me God" conclusion, Senator Fulbright smiled broadly and said, "Welcome to the Senate Foreign Relations Committee, Bertie."

I got a friendly send-off from the guys in the locker room. Everyone gathered together at lunchtime to pat me on the back and wish me well.

"You come back for a card game now and then," Jack Jackson ordered.

I assured him I would be back for a game or two, and I was.

The transition was a pretty smooth one. I made friends easily and went on to acquire a new set of advisers. William Hackney, the chauffeur for the Secretary of the Senate, and Bob Collins, who was Richard Nixon's chauffeur, gave me a crash course on the business of "how-to-chauffeur-a-senator," complete with practice sessions in the Senate garage on the proper ways to open and close the car door.

"First thing, you find out what side he wants to sit on, or whether he wants to sit in the front," Bob advised. "Does he want to be able to read while you're driving or not? Some of 'em just like to sit back there and close their eyes."

"If he wants to read, which daily paper does he want, and what section does he want to start with?" William Hackney said.

"Now, you could have a talker," Bob advised. "There are talkers and there are 'no conversation' people. You gotta find out what he wants and give it to him."

"But even if he is a talker, you remember you are there to drive," William added. "Speak when you are spoken to. No matter how close you and your senator get, *a chauffeur never starts a conversation.*"

I nodded my head, understanding all of this.

He shook his head resolutely. "Uh-uh. The only thing you say without being asked is: 'Good Morning!'"

There was always someone willing to help me. My buddy Preston Bruce, the White House doorman for many years and a fellow South Carolina native, took me aside to give me pointers on "how-to-drive-a-senator-to-the-White-House," including many dos and don'ts. The key for proper decorum, he said, was always to "respect the White House door."

"When you pull up to the White House and open the car door for your people to get out, you must help them out and then stand at attention by the car until they get inside the White House door," Preston said. "If they stop and talk to someone on the way in, you stand there until they get out of your sight. Remember, everyone, no matter who he or she is, is excited to get to the White House but no one wants to hurry in."

As it turned out, the Fulbrights were invited to parties and dinners at the White House quite often, and driving them there was a heady experience for me. Most of the guards knew me from my messenger days, so when I pulled up they would open the gate and wave me right in. I'd drive all the way up to the front door and then jump out, dressed in my tux, and open the car door for Mr. and Mrs. Fulbright, and then stand there at attention until they were inside.

Sometimes when I drove them to one of those special parties, I would stand in front of the White House and look down toward Pennsylvania Avenue. As the parade of senators and their fur-coated wives walked by, murmuring "Hello, Bertie" to me because by that time I knew many of them, I would think back fondly to the chauffeurs I'd watched behind the McDougal store when I was a kid and how awed I'd been by them.

"Bertie," I'd say to myself, "this is a long way from Summerton, South Carolina." Never in my wildest dreams had I thought that I would be driving Senator Fulbright and his wife to a White House party.

My main job was to take Fulbright and his wife, Betty, around to events, driving their individual cars or the car that was made available to him in the Senate garage. When I took the job with the Committee on Foreign Relations, I only had one car, my taxicab. One of the advantages of driving the cab all the time was that I could leave a little early on my way to work and pick up passengers to make what we cabbies called "the gas money."

I drove Senator Fulbright to the office every morning and then to his various appointments during the day. Sometimes I would pick him up from home and he would ride in my cab. Sometimes I would pick him up, leave my cab at his house, and drive his car. During the day, I often took Mrs. Fulbright to appointments to lunches and to the hairdresser, and since she loved hiding from the public, she often preferred riding in the cab. It served as a decoy. Their car might have been recognizable, especially to the prowling news photographers, but a cab was anonymous.

Fortunately for me, my taxicab became so important to the Fulbrights that the senator decided to secure a space for it in the Senate garage. We filled out all the papers with a special letter signed by Senator Fulbright that specified why a parking space was essential to the workings of the Senate Foreign Relations Committee. Incredibly, I ended up with the only Senate parking space reserved at all times for a taxicab.

One night after I dropped off the senator at his home, he told me to be sure to be in the office the next day at nine, as I was going to have my picture taken. I did not know what he meant because I already had a picture ID.

When I came in the next day, the Committee's chief of staff, Carl Marcy, told me to go to the Committee room and wait for everyone. The senators, who were members on the Committee, entered and took their seats. Marcy followed, and told me where to sit.

In the Committee picture? With the senators? I was confused. "Do you really want me in this picture?" I asked him.

"Senator Fulbright wants you in the picture, so sit here next to me," Marcy said.

I had forgotten all about the picture, when a few months later the senator gave me a copy of *"We, the People,"* a book on the workings of the legislative branch put out by the Capitol Historic Society. And there I was, in the picture of the Senate Foreign Relations Committee. I could not believe it. I had been employed by the Committee for such a short period of time, and I was already in the most popular book on the Hill.

I could not wait to take it to the basement to show it to the guys downstairs.

Now, this was the late 1960s, and things had moved radically from segregated to integrated to the era of the "token black." Usually if there was a group of whites, there had to be one Negro to show balance. Maybe I was asked to be in the picture because the Senate Foreign Relations Committee needed a "token black" face. There were no other black faces in that picture. I did not think of it like that.

I preferred to think it was because Senator Fulbright knew how much it would mean to me. However, no matter what the motivation, the photograph had a beneficial effect. A large framed copy of the picture hung on the wall of the Committee room in an esteemed space. I was told that whenever black students visited, it was my face they singled out, up there in the sea of whiteness.

"Who is that man?" the students always asked the staffers. The answer was: "He's Bertie Bowman, a member of the Committee staff."

If my picture made young black students believe they, too, could get a job on a prestigious senate committee, then tokenism wasn't totally bad.

And I absolutely cherished that book.

All the committees in the Senate have college students serving as messengers and interns as part of their staffs. Messengers receive a salary, and interns volunteer their services to get a foot in the front door of politics. Interns work summers and are often the children or friends of big campaign contributors. Messengers, on the other hand, tend to be bright college students studying in Washington, who work during the school year because they need the extra earnings to continue their education.

Both interns and messengers usually come from the same region or state as the committee chairman. I was not only Fulbright's chauffeur. I was also the clerk of the Senate Foreign Relations Committee, and as such it was my job to supervise the interns and messengers. With Arkansas Senator William J. Fulbright as chairman, most of those hired by the Committee came from the South, and all were white.

I sensed a lot of the kids were a little uncomfortable working with a black person. They were perfectly polite to me and did what was asked of them, but there were few of the normal friendly interactions staff members have with each other. Everybody knew his place.

The only exception was Bill, a thin twenty-one-year-old kid with a baby face and dark-brown wavy hair, who came from the chairman's home state and was a junior at Georgetown University at the time. Bill was definitely a mama's boy; the first thing he did after finding out he had the job was to call his mother. But that might have been because he was so glad to report the new income. He told me he had not known whether he was going to be able to come back to finish college at Georgetown, because his family did not have enough money. He had tried to get a job on the Committee before and had been unsuccessful, but this time, he told me, God had answered his prayers. Bill was very religious.

"I hear you and I are going to get along because I'm from the South, too," Bill told me the day he showed up for work. "Lee Williams told me you like people from the South."

Bill's job as a messenger was to go through newspapers looking for relevant articles, cut them out, and get them to the professional staff, who wrote speeches for Fulbright. He was a fast reader with an exceptionally good mind, and he really seemed to enjoy the work. There were times I'd catch him cutting articles from the Style or Sports sections of the *Post*. "Man, what kind of foreign-relations story can you find there?" I'd ask, eyeing him skeptically. But darned if he hadn't found a connection. I was his supervisor, but Bill taught me a lot as together we fingered through those newspapers from every state in the country.

What really made Bill stand out for me, though, was that he was not only smart, but he was good company. I could tell right off the bat by his warmth, his outgoing nature, and his comfort level that this was not his first time being around black folk. He was perfectly at home gabbing with me over lunch, not to mention enjoying one of Elaine's delicious ham-and-cheese or turkey sandwiches. He was both respectful and inquisitive, not only with me, but also with a lot of the older downstairs guys who had worked in the Senate for a long time. He wanted to know what their jobs were and, ever the history buff, loved picking up stories about former senators from them. Many times Bill could be found down in the basement "chewing the fat" with these guys.

He worked hard for me and in return, I cut him some slack when he needed it. The days after he'd been up all night writing a paper, I'd look the other way when things slowed down and he got into a chair in the corner and dozed off for a while. When he had a paper due or a chapter he had to read before class, I'd let him get it done first, because I knew he would make up for it later.

"Bertie, I got to talking with my professor after class and got so involved that time got away from me," he would say, gasping, when he ran into work a few minutes late. His being a little late never bothered me, because he could read and clip articles so fast that I knew he would easily make up any time he had missed.

We also had fun together. We had a little radio in our office, and we both loved Elvis. Whenever an Elvis record came on, we'd turn the radio up and sing along. His favorite was "Love Me Tender," and mine was "Blue Suede Shoes." We tried to dance along with the music, but neither of us could dance. One "slow work day," we got a bit carried away, and when Pat Holt, the director of the Committee, burst into the room he said, "No one invited me to the party." He laughed at the two of us—each with a broom—singing along with Elvis and pretending to be onstage. The word got around the office, and everyone had a good laugh at our expense.

Another time the mimeograph machine broke and we needed to get copies of an article out to the Committee. Mimeographing was the only way of copying back then. I tried and tried to get that thing started, but it wouldn't work. Bill could fix anything. He tore the machine apart and put it back together, and we were both ecstatic to discover he'd managed to get it to work—until we looked down at our clothes.

The two of us were completely covered in purple ink. It was all over my new suit, as well as Bill's shirt, arms, face, and hair. We mopped the floor, threw away at least two reams of paper that were soaked in purple ink, and received a lot of good-natured teasing from all the other guys, but still every time one of us looked up and saw how purple the other was, we started laughing all over again.

I had no idea that day that the purple face belonged to a future president of the United States. But it did. Bill's last name is Clinton.

SENATOR FULBRIGHT WAS yet another example of a southern segregationist senator who seemed to separate the political from the personal. He actively filibustered against the 1964 Civil Rights Act and voted against all civil rights legislation but behaved quite differently outside the hallowed halls of the U.S. Senate.

What's more, he had what appeared to me to be a fairly close relationship with Reverend Martin Luther King, Jr. A vocal opponent of foreign meddling, Senator Fulbright had become a focal point for anti–Vietnam War sentiments as a result of holding a series of Senate

Foreign Relations Committee hearings against the war. Reverend King was also against the war. I thought perhaps that shared opinion was the basis of their friendship. But whenever Fulbright spoke to me about King, it was the man's civil rights leadership that he mentioned. He'd be reading the newspaper in the backseat and I'd see him shaking his head and hear him mutter something like: "How in the world does Martin Luther King take all of that hate people put on him and continue to stand up for his cause?"

"Could you practice nonviolence like King in a situation like that, Bertie?" he asked me once. "Could you 'turn the other cheek'?"

"I don't think so," I told him, which was a considerably milder answer than he would have gotten from Jack Jackson and the other guys in the locker room, who liked to fantasize about training dogs to turn on their white owners. I was always a moderate.

"I couldn't either." Fulbright sighed. "I ask him often how he does it."

My ears perked up. "What does he say, Senator?"

Fulbright chuckled. "He always sends me back a verse from the Bible and tells me to read it."

BILL CLINTON AND I were sitting across the desk from each other eating sandwiches on our lunch break. "You look tired," I said.

"Yeah, I'm having trouble getting used to sleeping on a sofa."

"A sofa?" I asked him.

He nodded. "I just moved into a new place with a bunch of guys. Great apartment, only I don't have a bed yet."

"Can't sleep on a sofa, Bill."

"Oh, I can sleep anyplace." He laughed. "We lived on a farm once and—"

"You lived on a farm?" I shook my head. "I can't picture that."

"Well I did. A farm with cattle, sheep, and goats."

"I grew up on a farm, too," I told him. "We had a goat or two but mostly we had cotton, vegetables, and soy beans."

"Did you like living on a farm?" he asked.

I shook my head. "That's why I'm here. How about you?"

"That's why I'm in college!"

We both laughed. "So what are you going to do after college?"

"Go back to Arkansas. Get elected to Congress, maybe. I want to be a congressman."

"Not a senator?"

He grinned. "I may consider that after I serve a couple of terms in Congress."

"Well, no matter how you end up, first you have to graduate from college, and that would be easier if you had a bed," I said. "Now, Elaine and I happen to have an extra one. Would you like it?"

His eyes lit up. He followed me home that night, his cherry-red Thunderbird convertible, with red upholstery, trailing my taxicab closely. His mission was not to sleep on the sofa but to pick up the bed in his car so he could get a good night's sleep. Always generous, Elaine even added some sheets as a bonus. We put down the top of his car and loaded the bed. He drove off, all smiles.

The next day at work, he thanked me for his good night's rest. Also, his aching back appreciated the change.

ONE DAY SENATOR FULBRIGHT asked me to take him to the R. J. Reynolds home in upper northwest Washington for dinner. Since Mrs. Fulbright usually went with him to the Reynolds' home for dinner, and he was going alone this time, I assumed it was a business dinner. I parked his car in the driveway as I normally did and began to read the newspaper I'd brought along, when the Reynolds' butler came out and suggested that since it was so cold and rainy I might be more comfortable waiting for the senator in the warm, closed-in porch. I took him up on his offer.

After a couple of hours, the butler came out again. "Senator Fulbright would like you to come inside," he said. I noticed he was smiling but didn't think much of it. I had been a visitor to the Reynolds' home before.

This time, however, when I walked in I saw Mr. Reynolds standing talking to a black man. I took one look at the man's face and did a double take. *Was I dreaming?*

"Dr. King, I'd like you to meet my driver, Bertie Bowman," Senator Fulbright said.

A short, well-dressed man, Martin Luther King, Jr. smiled and extended his hand. "Good to meet you, Bertie." We shook hands and then hugged, and I told him how honored I felt to meet him face-to-face.

There were other people standing around, important people, I'm sure, but the only person I saw was Martin Luther King. He was the center of my attention. I couldn't believe this was the man who had almost single-handedly changed the course of American race relations.

Suddenly, a car pulled up in the driveway behind my car, and a man jumped out with a big umbrella. He held the umbrella over Dr. King as he walked him to the car in the rain, and they left.

The senator was ready to leave, too, so I put up my umbrella, walked him to the car, and opened the front door. Usually, when Mrs. Fulbright was not around, he always rode up front with me, so he could talk and joke. But this night was different.

"Bertie, I think I will ride in the back," he said.

I opened the back door and gave him the newspaper, and we set off on our way to his home. He was strangely silent, very pensive, within himself.

"It was quite a surprise, meeting Dr. King like that," I told him. "An exciting surprise!" I almost could not contain myself.

"I am glad you had that opportunity," he said. That was all he ever said about that meeting. He put the light on in the back of the car and read his paper. This was highly unusual—a first, as a matter of fact. He liked to talk in the car, and we usually had long conversations about a number of subjects.

As a driver, however, I knew an unspoken message when I got one. There would be no mention to anyone about who the senator had been with that night. Today the translation would be along the lines of "What happens in Vegas stays in Vegas."

Senator Fulbright's antiwar stance made him an anathema to the Johnson administration and the darling of the Washington press corps. Every reporter, it seemed, wanted to grab the senator for a quote at every opportunity, especially when he called for an end to the violence and a return to the peace table. As a result, Fulbright spent a lot of energy finding creative ways to dodge the press, and so did I, since I was the one who drove him everyplace he went.

There was the camouflage technique: the old wrinkled raincoat and black hat we kept in the car at all times, just in case. This turned out to be only partly effective. Half the time the senator was recognized anyway and ended up literally running to get away from the press.

No one loved outsmarting the press more than Fulbright's wife, Betty. Many a time we drove to the airport along a very circuitous route, as she had me going full-throttle through alleys and weaving in and out of streets in an effort to get rid of the cars of reporters and photographers following us. It felt more like an urgent police chase than a press chase, with Mrs. Fulbright shouting, "Left here, Bertie! Now take a right! Pick up the speed now!"

"Bertie, uh, don't you think we're going a little fast?" Senator Fulbright would mumble, watching the streets whiz by. "Think maybe you should slow down some just to be safe?"

"Oh, Bill, just sit back and relax a bit," Betty told him. "We've got to get to the airport, after all."

When I caught her eye in the rear-view mirror, she broke out into a big conspiratorial grin. Sometimes she winked, because the car's speed riled the senator's almost unflappable nerve.

Mrs. Fulbright's most innovative and successful ploy came one day when she and the senator were out of town together. "Bertie, do you think Elaine would mind coming along when you pick us up at the airport?" she asked when she called me at home the night before they were returning. "I have a plan."

She wanted us to bring two cars, Elaine's blue Chevy and the senator's car, which all the press knew by sight. His car was to be the decoy. "When you get to National Airport, park Elaine's car in the VIP parking lot that has access to that special entrance where senators get picked up," his wife said. "Then have Elaine go into the regular plane area. Bill will come out dressed in his wrinkled old raincoat with the hat pulled down. Have Elaine take him by the arm and escort him to her car. I will exit the plane from the back way, and you meet me there. I will ride with you in our car. Elaine will have the senator in her car, and we will meet at the house."

Planning such things was more complicated in the days before the introduction of cell phones! Believe it or not, no one noticed the senator coming out of the plane in his wrinkled raincoat and pulled-down hat. Elaine took his arm and they walked calmly to her car and pulled off.

The reporters spotted the senator's car, though, and stopped us and asked Mrs. Fulbright where the senator was. "Oh, he'll be out shortly," she told them cheerfully, keeping the conversation going until she was sure the blue Chevy had time to get away from the airport.

When we got back to the Fulbright home that evening, we sat down for cheesecake and coffee as a delighted Betty Fulbright explained how she'd come up with her successful plan to "fool the press."

THE TELEVISION SCREEN WAS FILLED with a banner proclaiming: SPECIAL BULLETIN! "Someone killed Martin Luther King!" the Committee staffer shouted, pointing to the television set.

We all stopped and watched in shock and disbelief. King had been shot while standing on a balcony outside his motel room in Memphis, Tennessee, where he had been taking a stand in favor of striking sanitation workers.

The news of his death was followed almost immediately by reports of violent reactions to his death in Memphis—shootings, beatings, bottle throwing, fires, looting, and police worries that such violence might very well spread to other cities.

The fear was certainly spreading in the Capitol as employees, black and white, began mumbling on either side of me. Two white women who worked for the Committee asked me to get in my taxi and lead them out of the city that night over the 14th Street Bridge into Virginia. They were too scared, they said, to attempt it on their own.

I did what they asked, but all the time I was leading them I was wondering in my cab what exactly they thought I would be able to do for them if there were any trouble.

Truthfully, I was scared myself. When I got back to North Capitol Street, I could see smoke coming from down on H Street; the skyline was ablaze with burning buildings. Fear filled the streets. Everybody was tense. I turned my car around and followed Pennsylvania Avenue east to my home.

This is crazy, I thought. Who mourns the death of a man who

believed so wholeheartedly in nonviolence by throwing bottles and starting fires? What's the satisfaction in burning down your own neighborhood?

The answer to those troubling questions turned out to be dismaying over the weekend that followed, as millions of Negroes in Washington and other cities began setting fire to the areas they were living in. We kept checking on friends and family to make sure everyone was okay. My father-in-law was worried about his business in the northeast part of town, but it turned out to have been spared. Even some white businessmen put up signs that said "Black Owned." There was mayhem and violence nearby, but it did not come out as far as our house.

President Johnson called in the Army National Guard and went on television several times to urge a day of mourning, insisting that nothing could be achieved by lawlessness, and urging rioters to stop.

As I watched Lyndon B. Johnson address the nation about the King tragedy on television, I thought about the enormous toll serving as president takes on a human being. Less than a week before, overwhelmed by criticism for his handling of the Vietnam War, he had announced that he would not run again for office. Now the man responsible for getting more civil rights legislation through Congress than any other president in history was watching as thousands of black Americans rioted in cities across the country.

It had all taken a visible toll. The lined, sober, exhausted-looking man on the television screen bore little resemblance to the yelling, cursing, brash, sure-of-himself powerhouse I had watched rule the Senate. He had visibly aged.

One night I was out driving Mrs. Fulbright on an errand, while Elaine and the senator were back at the Fulbrights' home watching the evening news and waiting for us to return. The commentators were discussing how they felt certain senators would vote on a Civil Rights bill that was due for a vote.

Elaine turned to Fulbright and looked at him questioningly. "When a very serious vote like that comes up, do you listen to your heart or your constituents?" she asked.

He looked at Elaine very seriously and said, "Whichever one bothers me the most." It was not a joke, notably at this time of grief and rage.

In the 1968 election, the Democrats maintained their majority in the Senate, but they lost the White House. After a year of social and political unrest, the country turned conservative, choosing what was considered to be a more stabilizing route to dealing with the war and civil rights. The Lyndon B. Johnsons moved out and the Richard M. Nixons moved in.

"You think things change over there in the Senate when someone gets defeated and a new man takes his job?" a White House butler, Sam Ficklin, asked one day as I ate lunch with him at the White House. "Man, that's nothing compared to the kind of adjustments we have to make here!"

"Like what?"

"We've got a whole new family to cater to—different kinds of food, different ways of entertaining, different shades of formality. Shoot, the ladies who clean say the Johnsons even liked their beds made one way, the Nixons have another way of turning back the sheets."

"At least you keep your job, no matter who the First Family is," I offered.

"You never know," Sam Ficklin said, shaking his head. "You never know." Then the man who had been a White House butler for almost five decades grinned at me broadly.

One of the Senate chauffeurs was, apparently, cheating on his wife and using the senator he worked for as an excuse, telling his wife he would be home late because the senator needed him, when, in fact, it was another woman who "needed him." When the truth came out, there was quite a scandal.

"Now, I don't expect you to ever use me as an excuse for anything," Senator Fulbright announced sternly one night after the scandal broke in the news when Elaine and I were eating dinner at his house.

I assured him I wouldn't think of it, but I found his announcement kind of amusing. I had no intention of cheating on my wife, but I could not have pulled it off even if I'd wanted to, because Elaine was with Mrs. Fulbright all the time!

The two women met at various social occasions and liked each other from the start. One Saturday when the senator and I had to go somewhere, Mrs. Fulbright suggested I bring Elaine with me when I came to pick her husband up. By the time the senator and I got back, Elaine and Betty Fulbright were off somewhere together. And that was just the beginning. Mrs. Fulbright was always looking for someone to go with her to concerts, and Elaine loved to go to concerts. Elaine found Betty Fulbright good company, kind, and very knowledgeable about all the things Elaine loved—music, art, flowers, and cooking, among other things.

Elaine loved to bake and knew her way around a kitchen. These women on television had nothing on her when it came to cooking. One Monday in January 1971, she baked some tasty lemon tarts and other sweets for a tea that Mrs. Fulbright was giving the next day for her friends. After the two women got everything set up on the Fulbrights' beautiful trays, they sat down to talk and chatter about Washington life.

"Elaine," Betty Fulbright said, "Valentine's Day is coming in a month. Why don't you have a party for the Foreign Relations Staff?"

Elaine did a double take. She was absolutely shocked.

Betty Fulbright was not a woman who made idle talk. "You know, the senator and I have been promising you and Bertie that we would come out to your home for dinner, and I think that would be a good time to come."

"But, we've been talking about dinner for the *four* of us, not the whole . . ." My wife was dumbfounded at the offer.

"Oh, Elaine, you know Bertie loves parties, and so do I! What do you think?"

What Elaine thought was that she was working at the center during the week and singing on weekends, and therefore, frankly, putting together a Valentine's Day bash for the entire staff of the Senate Foreign Relations Committee was the last thing she needed. She thought it might be too much for her to do.

"Did you put her up to this?" Elaine asked accusingly when I came home that night.

"Absolutely not," I said. "First I heard of it."

"She specifically said," in a perfect imitation of Mrs. Fulbright's voice: *"Bertie loves parties!"*

I was on the defensive. "Well, you know that's true. But that's *going* to parties, not necessarily *giving* them."

"Maybe just a few people will be able to make it," Elaine offered hopefully.

"Are you kidding? When you're a staff person on a big committee, you rarely get to even see the chairman. Fulbright wouldn't recognize most of the folks who work on Foreign Relations if he passed them in the hall. No one . . . no one . . . is gonna pass up the chance to get close up and personal with the senator and his wife!"

Elaine moaned softly, looking around the house and mentally cleaning it, going over every nook and cranny. She was already regretting it.

Mrs. Fulbright stayed on her from the careful planning of the menu, all southern food, to telling Elaine whom to call in the office to get a guest list. And sure enough! *Everyone* was coming to the big event, including spouses, since it was a Valentine's Day party. It was the place to be. Word was going around in the halls of the Senate that this was going to be one of the events of the year.

It seemed as though every night I came home Elaine was worrying about something new. She was constantly fretting over this or that, because she wanted this party to be perfect, to go off without a hitch.

"Should we tell the neighbors?" she asked me.

"Naw. Why tell the neighbors?" I was thinking that she was nice to be so concerned with them, but this was a closed event.

"You don't think they're gonna wonder why all these white people are parking their cars out front and knocking on our door?" She sat for a moment, wondering where we would put all the cars. Maybe police would be needed to handle the overflow.

I shrugged. "They might like to meet Senator Fulbright, I guess."

We decided to make it a neighborhood thing, but since it was a February "indoors" party and the count was already up to fifty people, there was simply not enough room to invite all the neighbors inside. Elaine came up with the idea of asking them to come to the front steps in hats and scarves, the way they did to sing Christmas carols, and greet the senator and Mrs. Fulbright when they arrived.

A huge, excited crowd was there waiting when my cab pulled up with the Fulbrights, and, like any politician, Senator Fulbright was delighted to have all these people lined up to greet him. The office had given me about twenty-five autographed pictures of the senator left over from some campaign, and I handed them out to the neighbors, who thought he had signed them just for them.

The staff members seemed to thoroughly enjoy getting individual time with the chairman, as did Elaine's father, Earl E. King, who was a big admirer and was thrilled to get the chance to talk to Fulbright in person. Accustomed to cooking for large crowds, Elaine made all the southern recipes Mrs. Fulbright suggested for the menu—fried chicken, potato salad, chicken salad puffs, and all sorts of cakes and pies.

In short, the food was a hit. The party seemed to be a success. To this day, we have no idea why, exactly, Mrs. Fulbright wanted to spend Valentine's Day, 1971, in the "ghetto" surrounded by Foreign Relations Committee staff.

I WAS WORKING in my office one day in 1972 when someone came up behind me and tapped me on the shoulder. "Bertie!"

The voice sounded familiar, but when I turned around and looked I had no idea who it was. I saw a young man grinning at me. He had long black hair, a mustache, and a long red beard. I shook my head.

"C'mon, Bertie, it's Bill," he shouted, "Bill Clinton!"

I hugged him, but then backed off and looked at him again. "Man, is that *your* beard?" It had been a while since I had seen him. He was certainly growing up and maturing into a wonderful young man full of promise.

" 'Course it is. I grew it at Oxford." He was grinning.

I pulled on it. It was real, all right. "Did you dye it red?"

"No, silly. It grew out this way."

"How does a guy with pasty white skin and wavy black hair get a red beard?"

"I don't know." He laughed. "It just happens."

"Get rid of it," I said, half joking.

"Aw, c'mon now, Bertie."

"Gotta get rid of it. You used to be handsome!"

He winced. "My mom says the same thing."

Bill looked around his old digs. I showed him how they dressed up our old office. There was a Foreign Relations Committee staff baseball game on the Mall that night, and since Bill and I had played together on the old Foreign Relations team, I took him with me to the game. Everyone was glad to see him but gave him grief about that red beard. We played ball that evening, and the team went for pizza after the game. Then I lost track of him for a while, and the next time I saw him it was in a newspaper picture. He was running for political office in Arkansas and he was clean-shaven.

"BERTIE," SENATOR FULBRIGHT SAID one day as we were driving to a meeting, "Do you still enjoy being in the Air National Guard?"

I cringed, thinking of all the times Guard duty had interrupted my life. "Not anymore, to tell the truth. They are always calling me up at times when I'm really busy with something else. It can be a nuisance."

"Well, then, maybe you should consider retiring."

That got my interest. "How do I do that?"

He wrote a name down on a piece of paper and handed it to me. "Go see him and fill out the form."

The next day, I followed the senator's orders and was released from the Air National Guard. Shortly after that, my outfit got called up again for active duty. I always wondered whether Senator Fulbright had known something I hadn't known, but the matter never came up again.

As we all know, when candidates run for office, they make promises. Those from agricultural states promise to improve the lot of the farmer, for example—to help to open up markets for their crops, and to subsidize those who are having a tough time. Those from industrial areas might promise worker reforms, while others vow to cut inflation and improve the economy.

Once these candidates get elected, they want to serve on the Senate committee where they'll be most likely to come through on those promises or at least look like they're *trying* to write a bill. The farm state senator might seek out admission to the Committee on Agriculture; the industrial state senator, the Labor Committee; the fiscal reformer, the Senate Finance Committee. Each senator gets to be on at least two committees, sometimes three, to prove to the voters that he is thinking about them.

Newly elected senators come to the Caucus Room of the Capitol for orientation and a meeting with their party leaders. This is when they formally let the leader of the party know what committees they are interested in, then the party leader calls the chair of the committee and tells him who is interested in being on his committee. The chair then meets with the rest of the members and they give the party leader a "yes" or "no."

To put in a good word for themselves, many of the newly elected go to the committee of their choice after the orientation meeting to make friends with the committee's longtime members in hopes of getting them to put in a good word for them with the party leader and the committee chair. They know where the Senate power is, for they are good learners and listeners.

I could tell Jesse Helms, the senator newly elected from North Carolina in 1972, really wanted to be on the Senate Foreign Relations Committee, because he hung around the area almost all day long, first meeting with one member, then another.

He'd even done his homework about me.

"Bertie, I understand we're both Carolina boys," he said, shaking my hand and giving me a hearty pat on the back. "I've heard a lot of good things about you from Strom."

"And he's told me good things about you, too," I replied, because, in fact, Strom Thurmond told me how much he liked Jesse Helms. With that introduction, another man with a reputation as an "archsegregationist" started becoming a personal friend of mine. "We Carolina boys have to stick together," Helms told me. "We Carolina boys have to help each other out!"

And, irrational as that may seem, we did. I really liked this man.

The other newly elected senator interested in serving on the Foreign Relations Committee that year was Delaware Senator Joseph Biden, who was much, much younger than Helms. He was so young, in fact, that he didn't turn thirty, the age requirement for senators, until a few weeks after he was elected.

Well-dressed and self-assured, Biden looked even younger than he was, but he possessed the confidence of a veteran politician. This caused a bit of confusion at one of the first hearings he attended. It was a "top-secret" hearing with the then secretary of state Henry Kissinger. Since "top-secret" hearings are for senators only, when I got everything set up, I went to leave the room. As I opened the door, the brand-new Senator Biden arrived somewhat late. Biden was a handsome guy with a lot of black hair who could have passed for being just out of college.

Henry Kissinger took a look at the kid entering the room and stood up. He walked over to the chairman, a frown on his face. "This hearing is top-secret," he reminded Senator Fulbright. "This hearing is not for staff."

Senator Fulbright looked at who was coming in the door and smiled. "Secretary Kissinger," he said, "let me introduce you to the new Senator from the state of Delaware, Senator Joseph Biden."

Kissinger was shocked. "Nice to, uh, meeeeeet you, S-s-senator," he said, stumbling over his words.

Meanwhile, the political knives were out all over Washington during this era of Nixon. "Democrats havin' a ball with this," Jack Jackson said, pointing to the picture of President Nixon on the front page of *The Washington Post,* boarding a plane with his fingers on both hands in the "V" for victory sign although there had been no victory. Nixon had been forced to resign the day before because of the Watergate scandal.

Jack drummed his index finger on the lead article. "Show me one place in that story that they mention the *real* hero of Watergate!"

We all grunted absentmindedly in the affirmative, too absorbed in the card game to respond.

"Well?" he challenged the group of us, "Who's the *real* hero of Watergate?" One by one, we looked up from our cards, realizing this wasn't a rhetorical question. The man was waiting on an answer.

"Who? You mean Ervin?" I replied to his question.

"Nope. Not Sam Ervin."

I shrugged. "He's the one who held the hearings."

"Hearings," Jack scoffed, his eyes circling once again. "This is not just about *hearings.*"

"The Judge," someone else offered.

"Judge Sirica?" Jack shook his head resolutely. "I'm not talkin' judges and senators, man, I'm talking *hero*! I'm talkin' an *unappreciated* hero, so by definition, I'm talking a man of *color*!"

Our eyes lit up in recognition and turned to the young black man in a security guard's uniform, whose newspaper photo was pasted up on the wall. "Frank Willis!"

"You got that right," Jack said, picking up a card. "Who started all this off? Who is the security guard who noticed a little, itty-bitty strip of tape holding that door unlocked in the Watergate building on June 1, 1972?"

"Frank Willis!" everyone roared.

"Who is the guy who called in the D.C. police to investigate?"

"Frank Willis!"

"Who is the guy who didn't even get a raise for all he did and is presently unemployed?" the guys called out.

Each of us took a deep breath, exhaled sadly, and nodded. "Frank Willis." The class on Watergate was over, with all of us getting a passing grade.

SIX

Drama and Decorum in the U.S. Senate

MOST OF THE YEARS WHILE I WAS WORKING WITH SENATOR Fulbright, there were endless election-night parties, but the most painful event of all occurred in 1974, the year Senator Fulbright lost the election. He had been reelected to the Senate in every campaign since 1959. The heartbreaking loss was a reminder to everyone that you cannot forget who put you in your Senate seat. One of the newspaper headlines said it all: "Internationally known Senator loses seat." He will be remembered in history for his firm stand against the war in Vietnam, but in order to win an election, he should have been paying closer attention to what his constituents in Arkansas wanted and needed from their elected official. Many political experts had predicted the loss, but it was still a shock to the staff, all of whom were assembled in Washington watching the results while the Fulbrights remained in their home state, Arkansas.

After the defeat, I picked them up at the airport when they returned to D.C. Mrs. Fulbright was madder than he was. All the way in from the airport, she was going over figures from the election, pointing out the defects in his support and talking to him about who did or did not get the vote out. When I looked back in the rearview mirror, I saw a senator with his eyes closed, emotionally drained, and a wife who was wide awake and talking nonstop.

Following their exit from Washington, the Fulbrights went away for a while, and after their return to the city they seemed more willing to accept the loss and get on with their lives. Mr. Fulbright went to work for a powerful law firm, and his wife went back to her daily activities. A lot of senators leave the city when they lose, but the Fulbrights stayed here. I continued to drive for them on weekends and evenings, and Elaine and I stayed in touch with them socially.

Senator John Sparkman, a Democrat from Alabama, replaced Fulbright as chairman of the Committee. He was older than Fulbright, quite focused, and less social. I drove him home frequently, but he and his wife did not go out much and when they did, they had someone else who drove them.

This turned out to be a blessing, because it freed me up to learn more about the inner workings of the Senate Foreign Relations Committee. I loved the freedom of driving the chairman and his family, but I also loved learning to be someone that the Foreign Relations Committee could depend on to run the very important hearings the Committee held.

My "professor" and mentor on the job was Buddy Kindrick, the Committee's chief hearing clerk. He taught me how to pull together the information each senator expected before the hearing: a packet that included the agenda, the resumes of the witnesses who would be testifying, the information on the subject of the day, the questions senators might want to ask the witnesses, talking points, and so on.

He taught me how to prepare for the press and public who would be attending, and how to figure out the most basic of essentials, which members on the Committee would want coffee and which would want tea. Buddy was a southern white guy from Arkansas and a friend of some of the professional aides. He was thankful for my help, and I was thankful for his knowledge. We got along fine, and I began a whole new career as an important cog in the behind-the-scenes preparations for the Committee hearings.

GOSSIP CAN SPREAD like wildfire. Gossip can take one fact and build on it until it sounds like the truth. Gossip can sometimes be a joke turned on its head. But sometimes it can hurt one's reputation, or worse yet, end a person's career.

Not many places could compete with the birth of gossip in the locker room. Talk was always lively, brisk, and on-target. We had many laughs about it, sometimes knowing it was not true, and sometimes not so sure at other times. But most times it always carried a ring of truth or, rather, it was the honest truth.

"I'm telling you, man, I saw him with my own eyes," someone said. "The senator was sitting there, all locked up in his car in the garage kissing Marylou."

The surprise was on the faces of my fellow workers. "Marylou? No! You talkin' about the Marylou who's on the cleaning staff?"

"Marylou who's on the cleaning staff! None other than. Like I said, saw it with my own eyes!"

Like workplaces everywhere, the Senate had its gossip mills. Stories were always circulating about who was doing what with whom, and one of the best and most accurate sources in the Senate was still the "basement" guys, the janitors and chauffeurs, who were often considered invisible by the higher ups and were witnesses to all kinds of indiscretions. Working the late shift, they knew who was locked in his office late at night with his secretary. Working the early shift, they also knew who came to work together, looking at each other lovingly in the morning.

"Your friend, Thurmond, had a baby by the maid," one of the drivers told me one day. He was enjoying the shock on my face.

I looked at him, frowning, with disbelief in my eyes.

"No big deal." He laughed. "He's always talking about how much he likes women, isn't he? He's not the first white man who had a baby by the maid."

"How do you know for sure?" I asked.

"The baby's no baby any more. She's a young black woman. She comes to town every so often, and I pick her up at the airport."

"He has you pick her up?"

"Yup. 'Bring her straight back here,' he says. 'If I am not around, tell my assistant to make her comfortable in my office until I get there.'" The driver shrugged. "Seems to take care of her. Gotta give him credit for that."

That rumor later proved to be true. The media got hold of his daughter, Essie Mae Washington-Williams, who came forward after Senator Thurmond died at age one hundred.

COMMITTEE HEARINGS HAVE always been theatrical performances. It was almost worthy of some of the productions on New York City's Broadway. Onstage, there was a V-shaped dais with the chairman accompanied by the senators with greatest seniority at the center of the highest platform, and the committee members with the least seniority at the far ends, Democrats on one side and Republicans on the other. Witnesses, who are scheduled to testify, sat at a long table, properly miked up, facing the senatorial dais. Behind them was the audience, the citizens who had come to watch the proceedings while the journalists and camera crews were assembled to report.

Part of my job was preparing the "theater." Once I knew the number of witnesses, I put the seats in position for them. Next, I figured out where the TV cameras would be placed in order to get the best shots without blocking the audience's view. I made sure the audio equipment would be accommodated, too, and that there was adequate seating for the print journalists who would be attending. I worked closely with producers of the media to get everything right.

Senate staff members, all specialists in the international area, would concentrate the hearings on political and social matters involving Africa, Asia, the Middle East, Latin America, and Europe. Known for their attention to detail, they did all the background preparation. These people wrote the "script" for their senator's performance, which was a document referred to as "talking points." Unfortunately, senators didn't always have the opportunity to read the materials the committee put together on the hearing topic, and instead received a quick briefing by a knowledgeable staffer on the facts of the senator's "talking points," accompanied by a sheet with those issues written out in quick, easy-to-read sentences. Expertly prepared, the senator would be good to go.

As with other theatrical performances, Senate committee hearings get critical reviews from the media. Some columnists make their living judging the performances of hearings and lawmakers. In the 1970s, a senator knew he gave an excellent performance if he was featured on the evening news in his home state or made national newspaper headlines.

Seniority is everything in the Senate, the ultimate power-enhancer. It gets you the best seats at hearings, the committees of your choice, and committee chairmanships. It even gets you coffee. If there is one cup of coffee left in the midst of a hearing and two senators request coffee, you can bet the last cup goes to the one with seniority.

Senators kid about this. "When I become chairman of this commit-tee, I'm going to fire you, Bertie!" Senator Biden often yelled at me dur-ing his early years in the Senate, when, because of his "junior" status, I attended to the needs of other committee members ahead of him. The threats to fire me may have been a joke, but make no mistake about it—all senators take this seniority thing very seriously.

I HEARD STEPS running toward me and felt a hand on my shoulder. "Bertie," Strom Thurmond called out as he rushed by, "Goin' home for the holiday?"

"Sure am," I said. "How about you?"

"Sure am too!" He grinned as he hustled toward the elevator. "Carolina boys always go home for the Fourth!"

I thought back to all those exercises I laughed at him for doing back in the 1950s and decided he had the last laugh. He was still a good thirty years older than I, but he moved a whole lot faster.

Senator Thurmond paused as the elevator doors opened and pointed his finger at me. "Ask around, now," he instructed, as he always did when I went home to Summerton. "See if anyone needs anything."

"I will," I told him.

Three decades after running away from home, I still returned to Summerton, South Carolina, every Fourth of July, along with hundreds of other Summerton fugitives. Traditionally, all the Summerton natives in D.C. would meet at a designated spot each year with wives, husbands, and children, and then follow each other down to South Carolina.

We no longer rented fancy cars to impress those back home, the way we had when we were younger. Those days were over for our generation. The fact is, we didn't need to show off. We all had good jobs and, even though things had changed a lot in Summerton, we were all doing better than we would have been doing had we stayed on the farms.

In 1979, the fourteen-hour sequel to the original *Roots* miniseries, *Roots: The Next Generation,* came out on national television, and when I got down to Summerton that Fourth of July, I discovered that my cousin Geneva had named her newborn son Kunta Kinte after the central character in the first miniseries, and another cousin, Blanche, had named her daughter Kizzy after Kunta Kinte's daughter—and *everyone* was talking about the television series.

"It's all true," my cousin Earl insisted. "You don't think our people were brought over here on slave ships like Kunta? You don't think . . ."

"Yeah, yeah, I know," another cousin interjected. "I'm just sayin' no man, slave or not, could take all that beating and abuse he went through and still keep going."

"Are you kidding? Of course he could! They all did!"

"Whatcha think slavery was, if not beatings and abuse?"

"What did your grandfather tell you? You don't think they beat our kin just like that right here in Summerton?"

"It was true," Geneva announced with authority, "because it was a *documentary.*"

That shut everyone up for a moment. I looked around the table with amusement. Nobody asked, but I was pretty certain no one was sure what a documentary was.

Ironically, the *Roots*-generated respect for their African heritage, and intensified anger at what southern whites had done to blacks in the past, caused my relatives to share with the white population of Summerton a deep-seated appreciation for South Carolina's senior senator.

It was an entirely pragmatic relationship. Blacks knew about Senator Thurmond's political stance, that he was the hero of the southern segregationists, but they also knew that stopping by his Manning, South Carolina, office could get their names moved up the list for jobs in a factory that was being built. It was a matter of survival, pure and simple.

My cousin Celestine, who taught third grade for many years in Summerton, told me about parents of her students who went right to Thurmond's hometown office when they got laid off from the factory. If they were good workers, Thurmond would find another job for them.

"If I am not known for anything else I do around here, I want to be known for helping the people who put me here," Senator Thurmond always told me. He kept his eye on the needs and wants of his constituents, the people who put him in office. And that's how he was known. I was surrounded by people every Fourth of July who knew of my connection to the senator and needed something, such as a job, a new mobile home, a license renewed, a birth certificate—and knew the place to get their needs met was through his office. They cared little about what he said about civil rights on the floor of the Senate. That didn't matter much to them.

Part of the July Fourth tradition was that all the natives who returned to Summerton got together at the Liberty Hill AME Church and stood up one at a time and said where they were from in the North. Each northern city tried to beat out the others for the greatest number of returnees. Church was then followed by a big picnic, with all the church ladies bringing their special dishes and the men tending to the grill where the hog had been cooking from the night before.

While we were eating on this particular Fourth of July, the pastor told us there were a lot of things that needed to be done around the church, but there was no money to get them done. When he left, we all decided to go home and do some fund-raising. That marked the births of "The Liberty Hill Clubs" in D.C., Philadelphia, New York, and Baltimore. The members of these clubs were even more competitive about fund-raising than we were about having the most returning visitors, as evidenced by the new church pews, hymnals, cemetery caretaker, church roof, and central air conditioning our funds made possible in years since. Almost in a biblical sense, the sons and daughters returned to the fold and the community was the richer for it.

SENATOR JACOB JAVITS STOOD UP when the hearing ended and glared at me. "I know how long two minutes is," he said angrily. "That was not two minutes."

"I can only . . ." I looked at him in puzzlement.

The senator was usually very even-tempered. "I'm not blaming you, Bertie. I'm just saying you need to check that time a little better."

"I will, Senator."

Each senator is allowed a certain amount of talking time during committee hearings, speaking on the chosen topic within the restraints of the clock. Being the "timekeeper," the person in charge of telling a senator to stop talking when his time was up, was not exactly the kind of job that endeared you to committee members. Some grumbled and others complained when their time ceased.

The truth was that Javits wasn't really mad at me. He was mad that he was a Republican in a Senate in which the Democrats continued to maintain a majority, able to put forth their agendas and get them passed into law. The time cut-off was just easier to quibble about than the Republican minority.

And quibble they did—all of them. Since time in the spotlight was something that was absolutely craved by all politicians, it was not easy and pleasant to be a timekeeper! Often, I would signal a senator that his or her time was up, and the senator would turn away from me, pretend not to have noticed, and go right on talking.

This created some serious fights. Just as little children squabble over toys in nursery school, so grown-up senators fight over time. Worse yet, they use time as a commodity, a bargaining chip, a currency. Senators bought and sold time as if it were candy bars. "I wish to yield my remaining two minutes to the senior senator from Illinois," a committee member would announce graciously, and it was then my job to monitor that senior senator from Illinois closely to make sure he took no more than the two minutes he'd been given.

And when someone "yields" his remaining two minutes, when, in fact, he only has *one* minute left, things can get nasty. Very nasty.

Then there was the problem of technology. What's the best way to keep time? A stopwatch? A computer? During the Vietnam hearings, someone offered Senator Fulbright a glass timer, filled with sand. "Best timer in the world," Fulbright told me, "after all, it comes from Switzerland."

If it was the best in the world, it was also the only accurate timer in the world because it never agreed with any stopwatch, mine or those examined continually by the senators to make sure my timekeeping was accurate.

With great relief, I abandoned the sand timer.

How do you tell a senator his time is up? A paper warning is often disregarded, as is a green light that turns into a red light. Trying to be subtle, I tried tiptoeing around and whispering, "Your time is up," but then it was hard to know if I'd chosen the wrong ear—Senator Charles Percy, for example, only wore a hearing aid in one ear—or if the senator talking simply chose not to hear me.

There were times I thought cattle prods might be most effective. Give them an electric jolt and then they would stop talking for sure.

IN 1978, Bill Clinton was elected governor of Arkansas, but then he lost the election in 1980. "I'm gonna run again," he said as we talked over lunch together one day. He ate a juicy cheeseburger, while I had the more ordinary hamburger, with a glass of lemonade for him and iced tea for me.

"Go for it," I told him, "I'm just waiting for you to come back here as a senator and serve on Foreign Relations."

"Congressman first," Bill reminded me. "And governor again before congressman. We have to do it step by step."

I winced. "That's a long time for me to wait!"

AS HE ADVANCED IN AGE, physical-fitness champion Strom Thurmond loved to invite reporters to celebrate his birthday by coming to take pictures of him as he did his strict regimen of a hundred push-ups. "How do you stay so fit, Senator?" the media would ask.

"I exercise, don't drink, don't smoke, and I like women," he always responded.

He often told me how happy he was that I, too, neither drank nor smoked. "The longer you keep that stuff out of your body, Bertie, the longer you'll live," he said, grinning.

Senator Helms eschewed drinking and smoking as well and commended me often for refraining from both vices. But Helms and I had something else in common: Neither of us had finished college. "We did all right for ourselves without that diploma, didn't we, Bud?" he liked to say. For some reason, he always called me "Bud."

The real bond Helms and I shared, however, was an aversion to exercise. Every lunch hour Strom Thurmond would run through the tunnel from the Capitol to his office. He consistently tried to get me or Senator Helms to run with him.

Ducking his invitations for exercising became a standard joke between the two of us. "Bud," Helms said to me when we bumped into each other in the hall, "I just saw Senator Thurmond, and he wants you to run with him!"

"Really?" I replied. "Which way did he go?"

"That way," he'd shout, and I'd take off in the other direction.

And we'd laugh a lot.

LEGISLATIVE ASSISTANTS, secretaries, committee directors, and all sorts of other Senate employees I have never dealt with personally have always come up to me and insisted that I "look familiar." I liked having them think that I looked familiar because I was famous, but in fact, I've always known it was really because I've had to be everywhere. My face was the one they saw when I was standing outside men's rooms, ladies' rooms, lunchrooms, and offices waiting to nab a senator in hiding.

This was the result of another one of my Foreign Relations Committee responsibilities—to make sure that there was a quorum present when there was an important Committee vote. To get a quorum, I found the senators in all of their hiding places and convinced them to show up in the Committee room, a task that is somewhat like that of a truant officer.

When I first came to the Committee, the job was simpler. I just went to the Senate bath or the barbershop to find missing senators.

By the 1970s and '80s, however, there was no Senate bath and senators had developed more sophisticated ways of avoiding me. Many set up small offices in other buildings where they could hide, not just from me but from everyone. These came in handy when they wanted to caucus with a few select others about how they were going to vote. A lot of senators maintained these secret offices, but few people knew where they were. It was my business to find out.

There were other hiding places: the lunchrooms of the Republicans and Democrats, the Senators-only elevators, and the places they liked to hang out close to the Senate floor. To get a quorum, I not only had to go to all these locations, but I also had to be convincing enough to lure them back to the Committee room, often saying "Senator, the chairman wants you to come to this hearing." What I wanted to say was, "You see me chasing you? Get over to Foreign Relations!"

There were lucky breaks, like the times when the senator in question was dying for an excuse to get away from a reporter who had cornered him. "Oh, there is Bertie," he'd shout, waving to me gratefully. "I must go to a hearing!"

And there were times, I must confess, when I overplayed my hand and gave them a bit of drama. "Please, Senator," I begged. "We need four more for a quorum and I can't find anyone!" Sometimes I did this although I really only needed one more vote.

"Bertie, you got me again," the senator mumbled when we got back to the Committee room. He knew he was caught by the Bowman net.

My record, however, spoke for itself: There was never an important hearing of the Foreign Relations Committee when Bertie Bowman failed to get a quorum!

IT'S FUNNY HOW you develop impressions of people when you meet them in person for just a minute. Former President Jimmy Carter, of Plains, Georgia, was the only president-elect we ever had testify before the Senate Foreign Relations Committee. After Carter was elected, the then committee chairman Frank Church asked him to come to discuss the Iranian hostage issue. President Carter made it a family affair, bringing his wife, his daughter, Amy, and his mother with him when he came to testify, and shunning all presidential fanfare.

I seated them and gave them tea and juice to drink while they were waiting, and Jimmy Carter thanked me profusely for being so kind to his family. Accustomed to brash, larger-than-life presidents like LBJ and Nixon, I kept thinking to myself, "This guy is just too nice to be president!"

In contrast, Alexander Haig, who testified before the Committee during his confirmation hearing to be President Reagan's Secretary of State, walked in as though he owned the world. We had a huge number of people lining up to watch the hearing because everyone thought it might turn into a confrontation over the role Haig played or didn't play in the Nixon White House during Watergate, but instead it turned into a forum on Haig's hard-line views on countering Soviet military power. When President Reagan was shot in an assassination attempt two months later and Haig delivered his now-infamous "I'm in control here!" statement to the press at George Washington Hospital, no one on the Foreign Relations Committee staff was very surprised.

OFTEN POLITICIANS CAN surprise you. "So, if you're going down to see your cousin Gladys this week, you should be able to make some progress on my lake," Senator Thurmond told me over lunch.

There were two bodies of water at the end of the Savannah River. One was named after Senator Russell from Georgia, and for some reason, Strom Thurmond wanted the other lake, the one that already carried somebody else's name, to be renamed after him. He knew my cousin was Gladys Bazemore, a civil rights activist in Savannah, who worked with W. W. Law, the man credited with desegregating Savannah. He wanted me to ask her to get the blacks in Savannah to say that they wanted the lake or dam or whatever it was to be named after him. I doubted I'd be able to get Gladys and her activist cohorts to go to bat on the issue.

—⟡ ⟡—

IN 1982, Bill Clinton was reelected governor of Arkansas, and he often came to Washington after that for governors' meetings, usually at the Hyatt on Capitol Hill. If Bill had enough spare time, he'd call me and I'd go over when they had a break and pick him up for our usual lunch—cheeseburger for him, hamburger for me; lemonade for him, iced tea for me. We had a definite junk-food pattern going there. He'd bring me up to date on his life, and I'd bring him up to date on the people we both knew on the Committee—who was still working on the Hill, who had left and where they'd gone.

On one of those trips Bill decided to take a bunch of his fellow governors to lunch in the Senate dining room. When he got there, he was told there was no room and that "senators have all the tables." He called my office, and I went down and found one of the waiters I knew, who then managed to secure a table for Bill and his friends. I had a good laugh over that.

"One day I'm going to be a senator," he hissed at me, "and then I will be able to get my *own* table!"

"Congressman first," I reminded him.

IN 1983, after years of political pressure on both sides of the issue, the United States Congress voted to make Martin Luther King's birthday a national holiday. In the Senate, the measure passed by a vote of 78 to 22, and one of the votes in favor surprised me. But not really. He had been a friend to blacks in his home state, but now he was standing up for a good cause.

"Thanks for helping get that bill through, Senator," I told Senator Thurmond when we had a quiet moment together.

"Time brings changes." He sighed, staring out the window. "Time brings changes."

I HEARD THERE WAS a retirement party for a janitor I knew who had worked in the Senate for forty years. When I stopped by the designated room, I was shocked to find the man sitting there with his family, all of whom had dressed up for the occasion, and no one else. I was so upset that I treated him, his wife, and his four children to lunch in the Senate cafeteria. I tried to make it into a bigger deal than it was, and they all warmed up and seemed to enjoy themselves. They might have even believed that lunch was the original plan, but I continued to fret. There was something about that empty celebration that made my blood start boiling.

I had long complained to Elaine about how underappreciated and uncelebrated the Senate's downstairs workers were when they retired. It bothered me on a personal level, because so many of these people had mentored me over the years—looking out for me, teaching me skills, and giving me advice along the way. They were the older generation who had raised me. They were my substitute family.

It bothered me on an employment level. Most of the downstairs staff sacrificed their time and energy to the United States Senate. Ever reliable, they worked long and hard, not only to take care of the Senate building, but also to attend to the personal needs of the senators, from shining their shoes to sewing buttons on for Senate wives who came to lunch with their husbands. After dedicating thirty or forty years of their lives to the Senate, I felt they deserved respect and a decent send-off for their committed service.

Of course, it bothered me on a racial level, since the downstairs staff was all black and the upstairs staff at the time was still predominantly white.

The lack of attention was especially annoying because the downstairs staff knew better than any other employees what kind of celebrations upstairs staff got when they moved on to a new job or retired. We knew because we participated actively in those send-offs. When I was a messenger, working with other messengers out of a "cubbyhole" in the back of a room filled with boxes, we were the ones who were called upstairs to set up the retirement parties for white employees who were leaving. We put up the chairs and tables in the hearing room or the reception room where the party was to be held, set out tablecloths, arranged real flowers in displays of beauty from the greenhouse, assembled the head table for the family, and placed the fancy china and silver that would be used for a meal cooked by the Senate chef.

These were big-deal celebrations, and many of them were just to honor some secretary who had worked in the Senate for ten years. We downstairs employees saw it all first-hand, dressed up in our gray blazers and burgundy pants as we seated the guests when they arrived and cleaned up after the last guest had left.

In contrast, when someone downstairs retired, no one suggested that we have a party in a special room. The cubbyhole was good enough. We just moved the few chairs we had around and one of us usually brought in some cookies and punch. There was no official send-off, no institutional celebration. No one on the upstairs staff planned anything, or even attended.

"Is it too much to expect that someone semi-official should come down and say 'thank you for all the time and effort you've put in'?" I asked Elaine one night when I was sounding off on the subject. "Or even 'good luck.' That would be at least a gesture of gratitude!"

I could not let it go.

"When a guy works forty years to make you look good, the least you can do is thank him with a decent good-bye!" I continued. "The White House sure doesn't behave that way. We know plenty of longtime work-ers at the White House who have been given memorable retirement parties by the First Family and staff!"

The downstairs staff who had retired or were on the verge of retire-ment began haunting my thoughts and participating in my dreams. I'd think about Vernon Talbert, who had been the black supervisor of the messengers, and Elsworth Dosier, who had Talbert's job when I was a messenger, and William Lowe, Jimmie Reed, and Mitchell Dorsey who had worked with me. I'd think about Oscar Quarles, Bennie Hoban, Mrs. Edmonds, George Johnson, Bob Collins, Hackney Williams, Bob Morton, Johnny Price, Mae Taylor, George McIvory.

"Take Wilhemenia Simms," I began. "She worked as a bathroom attendant for the senators' wives for more than forty years. Mrs. Simms had a little room off the bathroom, where she had a big sewing machine with all kinds of thread colors and buttons and zippers. She had make-up, hair stuff, stockings—anything a senator's wife might need in an emergency. And believe me, there were plenty of emergencies! Mrs. Simms came to the aid of many senators' distraught wives!"

Working in the Senate was a family affair for many downstairs staff. If your mother or grandmother or father had done a good job, you usu-ally got hired, too.

"I'm talking about multigenerations of the same family," I told Elaine. "Think of how many years of uncelebrated hard work that is when you put it all together! Take the Montgomery family, for example. Bill Montgomery started working at the Capitol selling newspapers at the end of the nineteenth century and continued working there for fifty years. His son, Ernest, worked on the janitors force with me and Jack Jackson, and then moved to the Documents room. He put in a good forty years. Ernest's son, Monty, took my job in the library when I was called up for the Cuban crisis, and he's still working in the Senate and Monty's son is about to be hired. Four generations' worth of dedication there! Isn't that worth at least a final handshake? A show of gratitude and respect?

"And they're not the only multigenerational family," I continued, pacing around the kitchen, getting a little carried away in my rant. "There have been three generations of the Queen family working in the Capitol. Lewis Queen, the assistant Wagon Master, and Edna and Bernie, who worked in the Linen Room. There is Elenore, who worked in housekeeping and Eloise, who worked in Senator Mansfield's home."

I sighed and shook my head. "I guess what makes me feel really bad is I now know how the other half lives. Since I started working for the Senate Foreign Relations Committee, I get invited to all those 'other kinds' of parties, and the contrast is so stark. I mean, if your family put in one hundred to one hundred twenty years of hard work, don't you think they should be—"

"Celebrated!" Elaine shouted.

I jumped. I guess I'd gotten so caught up in my own words, I'd forgotten there was someone else in the room. "Huh?"

Elaine shrugged. "I think perhaps it's time to have a big celebration."

"What do you mean?"

"Well, if you can't get the United States Senate to do the honoring, you're just going to have to do it yourself," Elaine said. "You can show all these people who took you under their wings and played an important role in Senate history that you appreciate all they've done. That we appreciate it," she corrected. She grinned at me. "Let's have a party, Bertie."

And so we did.

The guest list was huge, all downstairs employees who had retired or were about to retire after working decades in the Senate. Elaine started cooking soul food. Her sisters, Edith and Earlyne, did the decorations, and her brothers, Earl and Ernest, helped set up the event. The yard was decorated with pumpkins and beautiful fall flowers, hay and cornstalks. The grill was going with ribs, chicken, hot dogs, and hamburgers. We even served up grilled sweet potatoes and barbecued pig feet, everything that would make a backyard soul food party memorable.

And they came—some on walkers, some with canes, some in wheelchairs, some with medication, but they all came and had a great time. And, we hoped, felt appreciated.

As a matter of fact, the party was such a huge success that, by popular demand, we had another one two years later in our backyard, and a third party four years later at Hogate's Restaurant on the waterfront.

Throughout the 1970s and '80s, Elaine and I maintained our friendship with the Fulbrights. Unlike Helms and Thurmond, who enjoyed being "folksy," Fulbright was a brilliant man. He did not talk about pigs and cows and farms and being an "ole Southern boy." He talked about the issues facing the country and the world, and his intellectual presence was sorely missed in the Senate. "When all of us are dead, the only senator on this Committee people will remember is J. William Fulbright," Senator Frank Church said one day—to no one in particular, but to everyone—after a hearing.

Toward the end of 1983, during the Reagan administration, Fulbright returned to the Senate Foreign Relations Committee for the first time since he'd left office, but he sat this time on the other side of the "stage," appearing as an expert witness on United States–Soviet relations. Seth Tillman, who was the senator's former administrative assistant, accompanied him.

It was with great pleasure that I showed the former chairman to his seat and placed the nameplate that read "Senator Fulbright" in front of him. Alert and with a firm recall of the facts, Fulbright was seventy-eight years old, but as feisty as ever. "The Soviets are much more serious about arms control efforts than is President Reagan," he told the Committee.

When a former State Department official insisted that Reagan should be believed, and that the president sincerely wanted arms control, Fulbright quipped, "I don't have to believe the president. I know from experience that presidents don't always tell the truth." He then made several additional comments on "the idiocy of the arms race."

"I have probably looked forward to this hearing more than any other in my seventeen years, and I was not disappointed," Chairman Charles Percy said after Fulbright finished, and everyone laughed.

"You take care now," I told Fulbright as I shook his hand and handed him his coat when the hearing ended.

By 1985 both Senator Fulbright and his wife, Betty, were having health problems. After surgery, Betty had to go into a nursing home briefly to be cared for, and since he was ill too at the time, the senator went to the nursing home to be with her.

"Don't ever put anyone you love in a place like this," he told Elaine and me when we went to visit. "I have money and prestige and I *still* don't get the proper care in here. If I ever get back in my own home, I will never come to one of these places again."

The Fulbrights did manage to get stronger and back to their own home. The senator was up and about quickly and returned to work at the law firm, but Mrs. Fulbright never completely recovered. She insisted on getting out of bed every day, and she loved having visitors and gossiping. Sometimes she'd ask Elaine to pick up something for her at one of the small shops in Georgetown that she loved, and on Elaine's arrival Betty would ply her with questions about how everyone looked at the shop and what they were doing. Elaine felt the social information she gathered was more important to Betty Fulbright than the merchandise.

After a long illness, Elizabeth Fulbright died in October 1985 in her home, where she wanted to be.

"WELCOME TO THE SENATE FOREIGN RELATIONS COMMITTEE," I told the incoming crop of interns. As I began my orientation speech, I looked out at their young, eager faces and thought about how many times I'd given this talk and how many young, eager faces had passed through the Committee over the years.

Only one that I knew about had been elected a governor of a

state, but many had been elected to Congress or become diplomats or active politicians in their hometowns. I knew, because most of them wrote me notes every now and then to keep me posted. It was hard to tell whether working in the Senate had prompted them to go into politics or whether they'd chosen to come to the Committee because they were already interested in politics, but either way, they were a bright and interesting bunch. I loved that part of my job.

Away from the Limelight

WHEN MY FATHER-IN-LAW DIED IN 1989, ELAINE AND I HAD TO decide whether or not his limousine business would remain active, whether it would be profitable. The fact that the government was offering bonuses to employees who decided to retire pushed me in the direction of leaving and going into the limousine business, but it was a traumatic decision. How many sixty-year-olds could say they had been working at the Capitol for more than forty years? Not a one. But then, of course, not one could say he started working here at age thirteen! After many nights of debating and discussing, Elaine and I decided it was time for me to move on.

I am a party person. I love giving them and I love going to them, but I have high standards. I hate it when they are not done properly. When I told Rhode Island Chairman Claiborne Pell, who had assumed the position of chairman of the Senate Foreign Relations Committee by 1990, that I was retiring to take over my father-in-law's limousine business, my first follow-up line was: "I don't want a party."

And I meant it. I didn't want a fuss made over me.

Within a week, Sandra Mason, the protocol director of the Committee, told me that Senator Pell had assigned her the task of planning my retirement party, sponsored by the senators and the Committee's professional staff. Pell, she said, told her he wanted it to be "a big send-off for Bertie!" Realizing that if anyone could plan a wonderful party, Sandy could pull it off, I backed off on my protests.

And an amazing party it was!

Invitations were sent to all the people that I had developed relationships with in my years in the Senate—senators, staff, retired staff, State Department people, White House people, embassy people, nonprofessional staff, janitors, retirees, and so on. When Sandy received two hundred affirmative replies within a week, she said she knew then the party was going to be too big for any of the hearing rooms, so she went to Chairman Pell and suggested the Caucus Room, which was large enough to hold such a crowd. At the hearing that day, the chairman asked all nineteen senators on the Committee if they had any objection to having my retirement party in the Caucus Room. To this date, the only person other than myself to be honored in this hallowed room had been Nelson Mandela, the former South African president and leader of the victorious anti-apartheid movement.

They agreed unanimously to have it in the Caucus Room.

More than four hundred people came to the party, in attire that ranged from party clothes to work clothes to janitorial blue. I was overwhelmed by the tributes of some of the political bigwigs, including a few I had known so well. Bill Clinton, who was governor of Arkansas at the time, sent Lee Williams, who was on his staff then but had been a former chief of staff when Fulbright was chairman of the Foreign Relations Committee. Williams shook my hand and presented me with a congratulatory proclamation. Even President George H. W. Bush sent a letter of congratulations. I remembered the senior Bush during his days in Congress as an even-tempered, pleasant man who was kind to all of his support staff.

As you might expect in a room full of orators, there were many speeches, about twenty in fact, from senators. Some teased me, some praised me, some thanked me for the many small favors I had done over the years.

I still recall some of the remarks made at my farewell party as if it were yesterday.

"I'm going to be brief because I don't want Bertie to pull rank on me," Senator Terry Sanford, a Democrat from North Carolina, joked.

Chairman Pell called my retirement "the end of an era," adding that he didn't know how the Committee would survive without me. The others nodded their heads and smiled, and that made me feel very good.

Senator Nancy Kasselbaum of Kansas said she was grateful for the extra cushion I always put in her chair so she wouldn't look so little.

And some went on too long. "Your time is up, Senator," I whispered when Senator Strom Thurmond's speech showed no sign of wrapping up.

"Bertie just told me to shut up," he told the guests and laughed. "He's the only one here who can do that, because he has seniority. You know, Bertie was here at the Senate when I got here—plus, he is from my home state, so I guess I will sit down!"

Moments like those at the party amounted to a life's high points, important touchstones of one's years, and made me think back. Silently, as I looked around the glittery room filled with well-known and not-so-well-known people, my face reflected the gratitude and pride in a life and a job well done. I also wondered whether Burnet Maybank, my mentor, would have ever thought a party like this would be held in my honor. Probably not. But I hoped that the senator would be pleased to witness such an occasion and to know that, whether he'd intended to or not, he played a key role in my getting to this point of being recognized by all of those with whom I had worked.

When I got my turn at the mike, I did not forget all of those folks who had lovingly supported me—and they were many. First, I thanked Mickey for teaching me, the young boy I was, that doing your best was a goal everyone must aim for, even if you were sweeping the Capitol steps. I thanked the southern black imports to Washington, D.C., in the 1940s for nurturing me, answering my innocent questions so I could better perform the tasks awaiting me. I thanked Theodore "Jack" Jackson for educating me about race relations and making humor a necessary ingredient in my life. I thanked Senator Fulbright for sharing his intellect with me, and for his intuitive understanding of the things that mattered to me. I thanked Senator Thurmond for his guidance, wisdom, and friendship. I also thanked many people silently that night.

Before heading for home after the party, I performed one last ritual and invited Elaine to climb with me up to the top of the Capitol steps. I could not believe it had been more than forty years since I first ran up those steps. I stood there for a moment, feeling nostalgic and wondering whether life could possibly be as enjoyable without seeing the marble floors of the Senate again.

FOLLOWING MY POST on the Foreign Relations Committee, back in the 1960s, I found myself appointed to the Credit Committee of the Senate Credit Union. There were no other blacks on any of the committees at that time, and certainly none on the board. This was a very important committee because it was where members came to ask for a much-needed loan if they were turned down, for various reasons, by the senior staff.

Blacks had complained for many years about getting turned down for loans and having to ask senators to speak up on their behalf. I think this prompted Credit Union board members to decide they should have a black on the committee. When they asked me, I agreed to do it. It may sound silly, but at the time I thought back to all those lectures on saving money and the importance of budgeting that Senator Maybank had given me as a youth, and I accepted the position, in part, because I felt he would be proud of me.

Once on the Credit Committee, however, I became more and more aware of the racial discrimination taking place. I would see Credit Union employees stopping blacks in the hallways and loudly accusing them of not paying their bills. Blacks with good credit told me that when they wanted to buy a Cadillac, for example, they were told by the people at the credit union, "You don't need that kind of car; we will only approve enough money for a Ford." The Credit Union board could not have cared less about giving blacks a loan. It was just the way things were back then.

When I sat on the committee, I persuaded them to give blacks with "medium" credit greater opportunities to take out loans and at the same time, assured the Credit Union of repayment by having the borrowers agree to have payments taken out of their paychecks.

Gradually, I became the advocate for blacks with the Credit Union, and I worked my way up the ladder. I was first elected to the Credit Union board in 1976, and then progressed to the post of second vice chairman, then to first vice chairman, eventually to chairman of the Credit Union board in 1984. Senator Richard Lugar, who took over as chairman of the Senate Foreign Relations Committee in 1985, had been an active participant in the Credit Union for a long time.

When I became chairman of the Credit Union board, we planned a Credit Union Day to get more senators to become members. In this mission, Senator Lugar worked with me, and that year he helped me get twenty senators and their families to join. Each year when we had our annual meeting, I could depend on Senator Lugar to get other senators there and be the first senator to speak. We are not allowed to campaign, but whenever it was time for me to seek reelection to the Credit Union board, Senator Lugar reminded everyone to vote for me. It was highly unusual, but very gratifying, to have a United States senator act as my "campaign manager." He was very effective in getting out the vote on my behalf, just as he was on the floor of the Senate.

In retirement, I wanted to continue my volunteer involvement with the Senate Federal Credit Union to "look out for the little people," such as the tellers, cashiers, loan officers, clerical staff, and the like. One thing about it now: When you get turned down for a loan today, it is because you really do have bad credit, not because of your skin color. This credit union has come a long way in assets and race relations since I started on the board. We are now a $400 million credit union and I am proud to say that the board has had three black chairmen after me. Our senior staff is much more sensitive to the needs of its members now.

AFTER HIS WIFE DIED, Senator Fulbright began concentrating on the Fulbright Scholarship office, working there days and traveling to raise money for it. He tried very hard to stay busy. I continued to look out for him and called him often and stopped to take the senator to his doctors' appointments and special meetings. Frequently during our drives, he made no bones about the fact that he was feeling very lonely. "Bertie, I want to wake up with someone beside me," he'd tell me. "I want to stop eating breakfast and dinner all by myself."

Then one day, I got a phone call from a very chipper Senator Fulbright. "Just wanted to let you know you don't have to pick me up for that appointment on Saturday," he said.

"Really?" There was something in his voice that usually wasn't there.

"Yes, there's a very nice lady who will be driving me," he chirped.

I had the distinct feeling that the senator was no longer eating his meals alone.

On March 10, 1990, Senator Fulbright married Harriet Mayor, Director of the Fulbright Association, putting an end to his painful loneliness. He was eighty-four years old, and she was fifty-six. Their ages made no difference, not one bit, for they were perfectly suited to one another. Elaine and I attended the ceremony and reception and were delighted to see how happy they both seemed. He called me aside at the reception and told me that he felt that this was the best thing for him. I agreed heartily and wished him luck.

WHOEVER THOUGHT FUNERALS could be so lively? Elaine's father owned a limousine service, and since I was licensed to drive limos, I drove for him on weekends off and on. As his arthritis became worse, I began helping him out more, driving a second car when he needed assistance, and often substituting for him when he didn't feel up to it. I'd always thought of funerals as somber, silent affairs, but I quickly discovered they were only silent and somber if you drove the limousine that carried the coffin. If your passengers were alive, the chatter on the backseat could get as hot and heavy as at any other family gathering.

I felt the sincere pain experienced by many in the back of my limousine, but I also had little patience for the over-the-top drama queens, such as the lady who stood at the gravesite screaming, "Don't leave me, Bob! I want to be with you!" then got her heel caught in the grass and actually fell down into the hole on top of the casket. It took four men to pull her up and, man, was she ever scrambling to get away from Bob!

There is, I discovered, such a thing as funeral humor. Another time, when we were coming back from the cemetery, the family was sitting in the backseat sniffing and sobbing, until the guy in the front seat finally turned to his relatives and said, "What do you think Daddy would say if he was here right now?"

The others dabbed at their eyes in sorrow and shrugged.

"He would say, 'I don't know why in the hell *you* are so sad,' " the guy in the front seat said laughing. " '*I'm* the one who is dead!' "

Boy, did the family get a laugh out of that! They knew their father and what he would have said, making fun of the situation.

But lighthearted shared moments were rare. More common were fights over which family member had not paid his or her fair share of the costs, and complaints or, in some cases, praise, for the way the funeral home had handled things.

While the fiery "fair share" arguments remained in the backseat, complaints about the funeral home usually fomented back there and then bubbled over to me, the person they saw as the funeral parlor's on-duty representative. Often, I broke my number-one rule to defend myself.

The rule said I was not to talk to the grieving, even if they baited me. And sometimes they could get my goat, prompting me to speak out.

"I'm just the driver," I'd tell them. "I work for someone else. I don't know anything about the funeral home and the way it does business!"

Ironically, in the process of driving a limousine, I learned a lot about the funeral home industry in Washington, D.C., just by listening to the remarks made behind me. I learned so much, in fact, that then mayor Sharon Pratt Kelly asked me to be the consumer member— the only nonprofessional—on the Board of Funeral Directors for the city.

I think working for the United States government for so many years made me acutely aware of the power of politics, and not just on the national level. I had become active in local-level politics, especially in the District of Columbia, helping to organize a neighborhood organization set up to make sure residents got their fair share of tax benefits from the D.C. government. Neighbors of Burns Street, a neighborhood-watch group that started in 1979, met monthly and invited guest speakers from the local agencies to talk to us about issues that concerned us. The group is still active.

When I retired, I used many connections with the embassies in the Washington area, and our limousine business flourished on the jobs that involved foreign diplomats. There was only one problem. When the tour group needed more than one limousine, I owned the cars, but lacked the drivers. Elaine was a terrific driver but a geographically handicapped one. She knew how to navigate our neighborhood, but that was it. Sometimes I was forced to drive slowly so that Elaine could follow me. When she was delayed by a light, I would have to pull over until she caught up with me.

Once, we chauffeured two limousines full of Cambodians around town for a few days as they attended meetings, and when their business ended they all wanted to go to Macy's at Pentagon City to buy blue jeans to take back home.

"Pentagon City?" Elaine winced. "Isn't that in Virginia?"

I drove very slowly in the lead, but still Elaine managed to take a wrong turn. I drove more slowly, waiting and hoping. Still no Elaine. It was the time of the early cell phones, and they were not the tiny, svelte variety available today. Ours was in a really big case. You could not drive and talk with this thing. Elaine pulled over and called me on the phone, just as a group of police cars and a fire truck raced up the street next to her, their sirens blasting away.

Time passed as my palms sweated on the steering wheel. *What happened to her?* Eventually, I had to go over a few blocks to get her, and when I arrived, the backseat appeared to be completely empty. I trotted over and looked into the car. The Cambodian diplomats were all there, crouching down on the floor, their hands over their heads.

"What happened?" I asked Elaine.

Elaine shrugged at my question, puzzled at what she could have done that so frightened them. She glanced at them cowering on the backseat.

It took us a few minutes to figure out that the sirens screeching as they whizzed by had terrified her passengers. Despite the language barrier, we managed to convince them that they were not the object of the police hunt. But they were still nervous. Calmly, I led Elaine and our frightened cargo to Pentagon City. The trip ended successfully. We came home with two limousines full of blue jeans, but Elaine issued an ultimatum.

"No more diplomats," she insisted after that fearful mess.

STILL AN AVID CARD PLAYER, I continued playing in retirement but with a group that was very different from "the guys" who had taught me how to play in the basement of the Capitol. This group of lively seniors, consisting of about forty women and ten men ranging in age from fifty-five to ninety, is now a part of our neighborhood. They not only play cards but also feed the hungry, donate clothing to the homeless, plant flowers, and keep the street clean. They also play in pinochle tournaments in Williamsburg, Virginia; Hilton Head, South Carolina; the Poconos in Pennsylvania; and many centers in the Washington, D.C., area.

One year when my birthday came around, Elaine decided that just as mothers bring cupcakes to school on their young children's birthdays, she would surprise me by bringing a celebratory meal over to the center in honor of mine. She cooked the food, the staff decorated a room for the occasion, and the card players came up with a name for the group: "BERTIE'S GIRLS."

The center closed at three in the afternoon, and that disappointed the ladies and their sometimes male associates who always seemed to want to play "just a little longer," so I decided to invite them to continue playing at my mother-in-law's house nearby. My mother-in-law loved the company, and the ladies loved to continue playing. A trend was set as they met every Thursday. When my mother-in-law passed away, Elaine and I decided to keep the house available for the card players, and it became known as "The Bertie House."

SINCE I WAS NO LONGER a government employee, I was permitted to do something I'd never done before—campaign for a candidate. Following the senior Bush's presidency, Bill Clinton clinched the Democratic nomination in a crowded field of candidates with a whole basket of serious political and social issues. Shortly after the triumph, he asked me to participate in a Bus-Ride-for-Clinton being assembled for a tour through the country. I jumped at the chance. There were two trips. Hillary, his wife, ran the trip that I joined as an assistant. Bill ran the other trip. We spent a week traveling up the East Coast, with a large group of luminaries, stopping at senior-citizen centers along the way.

We'd start each visit with a speech by Hillary about the importance of getting out and voting, and then the rest of us would circulate a bit, handing out fliers, talking to the seniors individually, joking with them, and encouraging them to pose for pictures with the celebrities in our group, such as actor Tony Randall as well as vice presidential nominee Al Gore, and then we'd move on to the next stop. After all those years I'd spent with elected officials, this was my first experience observing a political campaign—what went into trying to get elected on the road. I loved it.

When Clinton was elected, Elaine and I attended one of the inaugural balls, but earlier in the day, while everyone else was watching the parade on television, I decided this was one inauguration I was going to see in person.

I went down early and parked my cab at the end of Pennsylvania Avenue, right where my friend would be climbing up onto the platform to take the oath of office. I had gone down there to see, not to be seen. I was dressed for taxi work in a jacket and jeans and was sitting there on the hood of my cab as the parade came by. I smiled as I saw Hillary and Bill approaching, walking hand-in-hand. They were waving at the public, at the people who had elected them. I shook my head, noting the twists of fate which life can hold as I witnessed that sight of the Clinton couple. That was a very exciting moment for me.

But apparently they saw me, too. I heard Hillary scream: "Bertie!" The next thing I knew, Bill was walking over to my cab to shake my hand.

My moment of fame was captured on television. While most of the people who watched the evening news that night probably wondered who the guy in cruddy clothes sitting on the car was, people back in my neighborhood knew right away. "Man," they said in awe, "The president came right over and shook your hand!"

EIGHT

Of Baseball, Boys, and Games

I N RETIREMENT, I WANTED TO BE PRODUCTIVE AND USEFUL, RATHER than just sitting in a chair and counting away the days. I didn't want to do that. I wanted to keep busy. I never stopped work completely, so I guess I was in semiretirement with my car service and volunteering with seniors. This was a time of change in my life. Elaine helped me to put my time to use around the house, which I didn't mind. But I was thinking about some of the younger people I'd seen around the neighborhood, skipping school, fighting with their families, getting into trouble.

I thought about what I could do to have an impact on their lives, to make a difference. I didn't want them to be victims of their environment. I figured they needed a mentor, needed someone to talk to, needed someone to believe in them.

For many years, I was a "Big Brother," spending a lot of time with our community's youngsters, sponsoring them on activities. I fondly recalled how the older guys had taken me under their wing when I first came to town as a shy, unassuming kid. They helped me greatly with their wisdom and experience, and I truly appreciated the selfless time they took with me.

With Elaine's help, I made our meetings and outings a family thing, just as I had that "family" setting with the downstairs staff back when I was younger. We took the boys to the movies, museums, bowling, concerts, baseball games, and community events. Education was a must on their program, too. I turned them over to Elaine so she could give them weekend tutoring to keep them on top of their homework assignments. Some of them thrived in their class work more than ever.

As a Big Brother, I involved the youngsters with the Junior Police program, so they could have the structure of an organization, and a pretty good one at that. The guys impressed them with their jobs of patrolling the community, preventing crime, and knowing all of the shopkeepers in the area. This was during the time when police officers had a different relationship with the folks in the neighborhood—a more pleasant one.

I had another idea. It involved baseball. I thought back to Mickey, who would pull out the sports pages that we read during our breaks from sweeping the Capitol steps. Mickey was a big fan of baseball, as were a lot of the guys around there.

"You can learn a lot from a sport like baseball," Mickey had said, folding up the newspapers, *The Pittsburgh Courier* and *The Baltimore Afro American.* "Sport, like life, builds character. Unfortunately, some of these folks are not learning anything from baseball, because we still don't want to believe that a man is equal to another, even down to playing a kid's game in front of people. It's unfair. That's what it is."

I knew what Mickey was talking about when he got mad about the color line in baseball, the colored playing one game and white playing another. Mickey often read to the guys from the newspapers, the black columnists Wendell Smith writing in *The Pittsburgh Courier* and Sam Lacy writing in *The Baltimore Afro American,* both trying to convince the white owners to let black players go to the big leagues. During World War II, Lacy was especially hard on them regarding the problem of barring the colored players.

Maybe the baseball bug bit me earlier while Mickey and the guys talked and joked about America's favorite pastime or when they teased about The Homestead Grays, the best team in the Negro Leagues, with all of their great stars. But the bite was hard and deep. I knew all of the statistics of The Grays, who topped the Negro Leagues during the Depression and war years, winning eight pennants and two back-to-back league championships in 1944 and 1945. The black baseball fans packed their home games at Griffith Stadium in Washington, D.C., while the white team, the beloved Washington Senators, was away. I never saw so many colored folks in one place, sometimes topping 25,000 fans, many more than the Senators, which usually finished in last place at that time.

"Imagine if the Grays or the Kansas City Monarchs played the Yankees in a series," Jack once said, thinking about such black star players as Buck Leonard, Josh Gibson, or "Cool Papa" Bell. "The brothers would whup their butts, even if they had the Babe or Gehrig."

Also, I knew all of the black baseball teams in the league by name, coaches, players, and their stats: Baltimore Elite Giants, Pittsburgh Crawfords, Homestead Grays, Cleveland Buckeyes, St. Louis Browns, Kansas City Monarchs, and the others. In the Negro newspapers, I checked to see how some of my favorites players were doing, with their pitching victories, home runs, runs batted in, and hits: Satchel Paige, "Judy" Johnson, Monte Irvin, Willie Wells, Sidney Bunch, Clinton "Butch" McCord, and Jim Zapp, to name a few.

When the Negro Leagues finally disbanded after some of the bigger stars were absorbed into big league baseball, I switched my love to the Washington Senators, although Clark Griffith, its owner, refused to integrate the team even after Jackie Robinson's start with the Brooklyn Dodgers in 1947. The pressure was on him but he would not quit his ban. Ironically, Griffith Stadium was smack in the middle of a thriving black neighborhood, located at Seventh Street and Florida Avenue, yet that did not matter. In fact, some people say Griffith's resistance to putting black ballplayers on that team hastened the loss of the Senators and their hasty exit from Washington to Minneapolis as the Minnesota Twins in 1961.

By that time, blacks in the city were fed up with the Senators. Our hearts started back pumping up with the beginning of an expansion team that same year, but they upped and moved to Dallas to become the Texas Rangers in 1972. Elaine and I were devoted fans of the original and new Senators teams, and spent plenty of time rooting for our city's ball club. She really got into the game just as I did, yelling and shouting for the players she loved.

One of my fondest memories involving baseball was when I was stationed with Willie Mays in the Army at Fort Eustis, Virginia, in the early 1950s. Mays was drafted out of the San Francisco Giants lineup during his rise as a star player in the big leagues. We became buddies and regularly played catch after chow. He was a friendly, down-to-earth guy without pretense.

BUT ONE DAY, something struck me as I was listening to a Senators game on radio. "Elaine, I was thinking about how much Mickey used to say you can learn from sports, about life and living," I told my wife while we laid out the dinner table. "Maybe the boys could benefit from that, too. We've got enough boys to do a baseball team. They would have fun, learn about winning and losing, learn about team play, and get out in the fresh air."

"Sounds like a good idea," Elaine said, smiling.

USING THE BIG BROTHER THEME, a baseball team comprised of the neighborhood boys was formed, and I soon thought that maybe I had bitten off more than I could chew. I would be a Big Brother to one boy and his mother would send all of her children to me. Sometimes a single mother used this as a way to get a man's presence into the boy's life.

I had to be a father for all of them, sometimes both boys and girls. I found that I was very good with kids, because they trusted me to lead the right way. Their ages ranged from five years old through to the teen years. They took advice, solved their own problems with my guidance, and most important, trusted each other. They asked questions about hitting, fielding a ball, pitching, and sliding into a base after a ground ball.

"Don't be afraid to ask questions, because that is the only way you will find out something," I told them. "Sometimes to master a thing, you have to make mistakes and only after making those mistakes will you know how to do that thing right. If you don't listen to what is being said, then you will keep repeating those mistakes. Baseball's just like life."

To spark things up, Elaine made a cheering squad out of the girls, whose yells and shouts of encouragement made everything just right. While the boys played baseball, the girls, with the parents as well, cheered us on, and when the game was finished, we dined on cookies and glasses of punch as a treat. Everything was perfect for our team and their games, since we lived across the street from a big park that had a baseball field, a football field, basketball courts, and a swimming pool. All I had to do was to reserve the baseball field when games were scheduled, and that was that.

As a coach, I didn't have to motivate them. There was nothing official. We weren't a part of any league because we just played each other. In fact, I don't think we got around to naming the team. Sometimes the neighborhood kids would join in the fun with our ragtag team, but we had a ball on that park field with its makeshift bases and tall grass. I was never shy about telling them how proud I was of them for making a good catch, striking out batters, or pulling off a crazy double play. I couldn't have been prouder of them if they were my own kids.

The other thing was that the parents didn't want me to "fix" their kids or save them. In that park, all they wanted their youngsters to do was play and have fun, although sometimes we would laugh when they made fielding errors or swung at a pitch two or three times before it went into the catcher's glove. It was all lighthearted fun, with no tension or pressure.

"I love what you're doing with these kids around here," one of the parents would say, grinning from ear to ear. "Keep it up. We need something like this so they won't get into trouble. God bless you and Elaine." That made me feel great. It made my day.

At least twice a month we took the whole baseball team to the big league games in Baltimore, and they loved it. We made an event of it, a big trip, with ten or fifteen kids packed like sardines into our old limousine. When the neighborhood kids heard about our trips, I arranged to pick them up in my car, and they crowded into my backseat with their faces pressed against the car's windows.

I knew all of these neighborhood youngsters, both good and bad. Some of them had something missing from their lives—no father, a mother who drank, or living with grandparents too old to give them proper attention. Trouble was only minutes away. Nobody gave them a safe, caring way to live or survive in this real world. They didn't have the chance that I had when I left home to come to the city back then. I guess I had been lucky in more ways than one, by meeting the people I met and having the opportunities I had when I was young.

On the trip, we pulled both cars into the parking lot near Memorial Stadium in Baltimore and then lined up to enter the crowded ballpark. We had to make sure that everyone was present and accounted for, so Elaine would count heads before we found our seats in the bleachers. The tickets were cheap, around two dollars each, not like today. It costs an arm and a leg to get good seats now. One thing we enjoyed about going to the games in those days was that we could cook lots of hot dogs at home, put them in a wide-mouthed thermos, and bring along the rolls, mustard, and relish. Yum, good eating!

Not only would I explain the mechanics of baseball to the kids, but I would always include the themes of life and what they could expect when they became grown up. Sometimes we would have a whole row of kids. Elaine loved to hear me talking to them as a coach, mentor, and substitute father.

After the trip was over, we dropped the youngsters off at their homes, all tired but content that we had done a very good thing. Elaine saw the satisfied smile on my face and winked, taking my hand, and we sat in the living room, completely happy.

"The kids can sure tucker you out," I said, resting my feet.

Elaine knew how much fun it was for me to take the youngsters to a big league game, since it gave me a chance to feel like a father. I had no children with me, and that was a major regret. Still, we knew we were making a difference in their lives and that these games and trips would probably stick with them for the rest of their days.

The Difference Between
the Personal and the Political

W HAT A DIFFERENCE TEN YEARS MAKES! BEFORE I KNEW IT, A decide had passed since I'd retired from my post at the Senate. Although Barbara Allem, the chief clerk, had called me several times to help with hearings during that time, I never thought I would come back on a daily basis. One day, Barbara and her husband, Johnny, had my wife and me over for dinner, and I could tell that my friend wanted to know if my retirement was permanent. From the dinner conversation, I realized that she and Senator Helms had been discussing my comeback.

In the middle of the meal, Barbara, my petite, soft-spoken friend, popped the question: "Would you come back to work if the senator asked you, Bertie?"

I laughed and immediately said, "Yes." I thought nothing about it until my phone rang a few days later.

"How are ya doing, Bud?" the familiar Southern accent boomed at me through the telephone receiver. I recognized the voice of my friend from its rural twang. I had been in retirement for a while but I was restless.

"I'm doing just fine, Senator. How are you doing?"

"I'm okay," Senator Jesse Helms replied. "I was just wondering if you might be getting a little tired of being retired."

"Well . . ." I replied. "You were?" He had a point, but retirement had treated me right.

The senator spoke so clearly that it was as if he were in the next room. "Yes. You know, it finally happened. They made me Committee chairman. So how about coming back to the Committee as my Hearing Coordinator?" he asked me.

My heart missed a beat. "You want . . ."

His voice went up when he answered me. "You! I want you. Told you when I got to be chairman that I'd be calling you back to work! I'm gonna be holding hearings at the United Nations in January, a first for the Senate Foreign Relations Committee, and I want them to go smoothly. There's only one person I know who can make that happen. What do you say, Bud?"

I had been retired for ten years. I had been busy. I had been productive. Life was good, but I sorely missed my favorite place in the world. Coordinating a Committee hearing at the United Nations sounded like an exciting challenge. "That's awfully . . ."

The senator knew the proper protocol for any decision, and that was getting the nod from my wife. "Now, you see if this is all right with Elaine first, and then get back to me."

I could not control myself when I hung up that phone. I was so happy. It would be good to be back in the saddle again. I was surprised by how much I had missed the whole political scene.

Instead of phoning Senator Helms back, I just showed up in his office the next morning and told him I was as excited about holding hearings at the United Nations as he was. He sat me down and went over the details: which Committee members would be traveling to New York for the hearings, who would be giving speeches, and so on. "I'd like you to come back and supervise the Committee interns, too," he said. "Give them the benefit of your knowledge of the Capitol and the Senate Foreign Relations Committee. You always did such a good job with them."

"When do you want me to start?"

"How about right now?" He held out his hand. "Welcome back, Bud!"

Back on the job, things had changed. So many of the senators I'd worked with back in 1990 had retired, and so had most of the downstairs staff. What's more, most of the janitorial jobs blacks held before were now held by Hispanics. I used to love to go down to the locker room and chat with the guys, or head over to the cafeteria and talk to some of the women who worked there, but that was not the case in 2000—I would have to speak Spanish.

I was shocked to walk the familiar Senate halls and not see anyone I knew. Even more shocking to my ego was the fact that no one knew me! I was the invisible man. I'd always prided myself on knowing everyone around that building, including the police force, but when I drove up to the Senate garage, there was not a single familiar face on the gate. A whole new security crew manned the barrier. Times had indeed changed.

A young, eager policeman stuck his head in the window of my cab. "You cannot come in here, sir," he said in a very authoritative voice. "No taxis are allowed in the garage." Barbara had warned me this was going to happen and had prepared me with all of the documents needed to get into the garage.

The policeman looked at them and told me to pull over to the side. He got on his radio and called his supervisor, and before long several of them were standing around my taxi. Finally, a man with the most decorations on his shirt came after much fanfare and called the Foreign Relations Committee, and then my cab was permitted to enter the garage.

In my time away from the Senate, the Committee Hearing Room, too, had received a bit of an overhaul, with new chairs and a new seating arrangement, but there, at least, I felt at home. This was my arena, a place to be in charge, and I felt just as comfortable in that room as I had ten years before.

Senator Helms, of course, made sure he introduced me to every senator on the Committee as well as to any who happened to pass us in the halls. "This is Bertie Bowman," he liked to say, a twinkle in his eye. "Bertie was Bill Clinton's boss."

I would have liked to think the line was an attempt on Helms's part to boost my importance, but instead I felt it was intended to be a put-down of a president whose political views Helms did not share.

Unsure how to behave with that kind of introduction, I decided to just "go with the flow." I held out my hand the way a man quali-fied to be "Bill Clinton's boss" would and said, "Glad to meet you." I was amused, however, at some of the quizzical stares I received from diplomats from other countries who did not know what to think. However, those diplomats were very polite and pleasant upon our meeting.

THE NOTION OF creating a notable legacy was important in any public official's life at that time and still is now. Thurmond, Helms's buddy, was aiming at being the oldest working senator, persevering in his reign through all incoming administrations, Democratic and Republican. His physical workouts would serve him well. However, Helms wanted to be the first chairman of a committee to have a Con-gressional hearing in the United Nations, an event of some prestige in Washington and around the world. I think he figured that telling off the United Nations in a public spotlight was not a half bad swan song. To continue Helms's political legacy, I made it a point during my orientation session on the history of the Committee to tell the interns that Senator Helms chaired the first U.S. Senate Committee on Foreign Relations hearing before the United Nations Security Council.

"Remember this fact," I jokingly told them. "You never know, it may be the final question on *Jeopardy!,* and if you know the answer you can win enough money to pay off your student loans!"

Satisfied with his triumph at the U.N., Helms was very con-tent when we returned from New York, and so was I. It was great after ten years in retirement to know I could still do the job. And it was a great honor to be asked. But more important than this U.N. hearing was that I had missed my old "home" and being useful in the U.S. Senate.

Senator Helms was always a "people person." He really loved being around a group of people who wanted to talk politics, and he also loved to stir up the political minds of young people. He often took time out for discussions with the interns on the Committee, loving the exchange of ideas. As he got older, though, he retreated from the spotlight, withdrawing to spend private time with his wife and depending on me to drive him around more and more. I took him and Mrs. Helms to parties at the White House and elsewhere around town. I got to know his two daughters and granddaughters, and gradually they included Elaine and me in many of their social events. Often we were the only black couple there, but the truth was we were, and still are, the only blacks at most of the functions we go to that are sponsored by senators, the Capitol, or the White House.

Needless to say, Helms was a thoughtful host. He always had us seated at his table and explained our presence casually to everyone there.

"Bertie works with me on the Foreign Relations Committee," Helms said to those gathered nearby. "He's a very useful man to all our operations."

I never discussed with Senator Helms the terrible things he said about blacks over the years on the campaign trail or how he had managed his narrow defeat of Harvey Gantt, a black political opponent trying to take his seat. Nor did I discuss some of the negative things he'd said publicly about my friend Bill Clinton. I dealt with him on a very personal, one-on-one level, and on that level he was a good friend who treated me with respect, attentively noticing the work I did and praising me for it. I never had to wonder if he really appreciated me because he always told me, both when we were alone and in front of a room full of people.

"Bud, thank you again for the way you ran that committee today," he'd say at the end of a hearing. "I would not look so good if I did not have you to help run things for me." And he seemed very sincere.

And I was not the only black person who felt that way. He talked to me often about the blacks he had hired at his radio station. Many came to visit him in Washington and Helms introduced me to them. They seemed to like him personally as much as I did. Ahh, the difference between the personal and the political.

Senator Helms also knew how to throw a great party, and you know I love to party. One event that Elaine and I will never forget was the Helms Family Reunion in North Carolina, a huge celebration for everyone who was related to the family or had worked for Jesse Helms. Being the gracious host, Helms put all those invited up at a five-star hotel in Carey, North Carolina. People came from all over the world for this reunion, and we took up the whole hotel. We were given an agenda for the weekend, and when it was time for an event a bus picked us all up at the hotel and took us away to a different part of the countryside.

I knew about half the people who were invited, because they were either family members or staff people who had worked in the Senate or his home office. There were champagne toasts, seven-course meals and barbecues at the ranches, dancing under the stars and concerts in outdoor theaters. This went on for at least four days. It was the most wonderful weekend Elaine and I had ever attended. The food was lavish and delicious, and the setting changed every night, as did the entertainment.

It was fitting that when Jesse Helms retired and left Washington, he threw yet another great party, this one an incredible farewell party. Many politicians were there to toast him. President George W. Bush was out of the country, but they showed a film in which the president told Helms how much he would miss him. As we were leaving, reporters from the *Washington Post* and the *Hill* rushed up to me and asked me why I was there.

"Because I was invited," I told them.

"How do you know Senator Helms?" they asked.

I let them hold their breath before I answered. "I worked for him, and we have been friends for many years."

Then the question I'd been waiting for came from one of the reporters. "How can you be a friend of Jesse Helms when he has voted consistently to hold black people back?"

"Jesse Helms has his political agenda and I have mine." I shrugged. "He has a right to his views and I have a right to mine."

When the reporters walked away, I thought that was the end of it, but I found myself quoted in the newspaper the next day. I'm sure that Senator Helms saw the newspaper but neither of us ever spoke of it. We remain close friends until this day, for we respect each other not only as men but human beings.

TEN

Summerton Then and Now

SOMEBODY SAID YOU CAN'T GO HOME AGAIN. BUT THE GOOD BOOK says that is false because you should make friends with your past or it will get the best of you. I remember that first trip back home to Summerton, and how I dreaded it. With some prodding from Mrs. Johnson, my landlady at the time, I started feeling good about going home, feeling my mama's soft lips against my cheek, and searching my daddy's eyes for a reason to let him into my heart.

Summerton represents the distance I have come, from the scared young boy at the bus station, doubting my ability to go any farther. Maybe the Old South was built to make you doubt yourself, make you feel that you couldn't measure up to other people. Sometimes I wonder how I did it, made that tough journey across the color line to the city and a job at the Capitol Building. I could have taken another path and ended up somewhere else. But that was not to be.

Everybody always harps on the bitter, painful memories of the past. If we have those recollections of the Old South during slavery and Jim Crow, we have got to get on past them. If we have some disdain for the white folks and their deeds, we have to let it go, get on past it, and go on to thrive and prosper as a family and community. I'm reminded of an old Negro man, whom I respected not only because of his age and courage but because of his determination, in my adopted city.

"We have to forgive our men for what they didn't say and didn't do during those awful times," the old man said, looking at me through his thick eyeglasses. "They did all they could under some really bad situations. We must forgive them because they gave us life and the boldness to survive. If it was not for them, we would have been finished."

As the old man walked away from me, he whispered to me that hopelessness was not in their language. They always had that inner courage. I know I had it when I ran away from home. I believed in myself, in the possibility of my future, and knew I had the right upbringing to build a good life in any place. But I knew I would always return home like the sons and daughters who would borrow, beg, and go into hock so they would have new clothes and cars upon their return from the North, because the notion of home was very important to them and the love and approval of their families and relatives.

As I drove through Summerton recently I felt it was home. This was family. Sure, Summerton always seemed as though it was in a time machine, reluctant to change, but it was moving forward slowly and quietly. With a population of barely over a thousand, the small country town didn't have a big-time college or a library. On the road, I could see the empty lots of land marked for new construction, though what they were putting there was a mystery. The large trailer homes, the shanties with the tin roofs, and the shuttered storefronts on the town's main street said hard times were still gripping the folks in the area.

Certainly, most of the main roads are paved now, yet the majority of the back ones remain dusty dirt roads. The Summerton folks have street names and street signs in some places, with several of them named after longtime families in the area. This means that some of the street signs have black family names. I was really surprised that they have a paved road between Summerton and Manning named after Althea Gibson, the black woman tennis great. The place is marked with a plaque, saying that she grew up on that road.

"What's the difference in Summerton between today and yester-day?" I asked some family members gathered in what was our old yard.

My brother Larry smiled and replied: "Nothing's changed. It's still the same. It still doesn't have a McDonald's." That always got a laugh.

One good thing about Summerton is that many of the black farm-ers have managed to hold on to their farms and surrounding land, un-like many places in the South. I can think of several black families who have worked the land for a long time, such as the McDonalds, the Blackwells, and the Richardsons. They put their profits back into their farms so they could sustain their spreads.

I remember all those hot summer days when the menfolk dragged themselves home from the fields, completely tired and just wanting to get some food in them and have a good night's sleep. We children would still laugh and play among ourselves, for it was a very simple time then. But now I wondered what the youngsters did to have fun. Look-ing around in Summerton, it seems there was nothing to do and no place to go.

As I sat in the car, I watched Summerton's black youngsters and wondered if they had the same dreams I did. I didn't want them to be wrapped in hate, frustration, and confusion. They gathered like young birds, laughing, joking, and teasing each other, but I sensed something was missing. It was in their eyes, the way they held their bodies, even the way they talked to each other. In this place, sometimes they are not allowed to be children and are hurried to become grown-ups, speak their minds, and stand up for themselves. That is not good. Youngsters should be able to enjoy their youth, for this is a time that only happens once. I was not permitted to be a kid. It seems that I was always a grown-up even when I was wearing short pants.

Traveling around Summerton, I made sure that I stopped by all the folks who knew me and wished me well. They didn't give me a hero's welcome but treated me like any other person. That type of greeting made me feel important, like I belonged here, like I was one of the folks. Never had I known such kindness and respect. They greeted me with warm words, sincere smiles, happy grins, and pats on the shoulder and back. As I said, so much of Summerton has changed, but a lot of things have not changed. Both of the houses I lived in with my family have been torn down. When I stood there, it was all open field and tall grass. My memory of those houses is just as clear as when I first set foot in them—I can remember the creak of the wooden floors, the cold wind coming through the cracks in the windows, and the delicious aroma of Mama's cooking. Well, the oak tree is still there, strong and robust.

Over the years, Summerton has meant more to me than I had realized. Home. Home was much more than a roof over your head. It represented the love, support, comfort, and commitment of family and friends. I never took my loving, caring family for granted, unlike some other folks. I always went the extra mile to meet them on common ground, always showing them the love, respect, and gratitude they deserved.

For most black people, family reunions are an occasion to celebrate the generations, from the lap babies to the experienced elders. I try to make it to every reunion I can, for I love the old folks, young folks, great-aunts and -uncles, cousins, nephews—everyone. It's like one big party. What I love is that the elders try to pass on the history of the clan to the young ones, noting the successes and achievements of those who came before them. That sturdy family tree. I have a healthy respect for them, because I know they gave me the gifts of their wisdom and experience so I could build a better life for myself.

"All they want is for you to be a man," an uncle of mine said at one of the reunions.

"Keep control of your heart and your head. Don't think too much. Don't complain too much. Weigh your choices carefully. Just believe that everything will work out in the end. Never allow anyone to make decisions for you. And never be afraid of failure, because it will make success that much sweeter."

I love being around family, because you get tidbits about your past and bloodline that you would have never known. Sometimes I look at the photos of the various reunions taken over the years, and see familiar faces, memorizing what they said or did. Some of the photos I know by heart, having tucked them away in my mind's eye. However, there are three souls I want to single out, for I appreciated them more and more with each passing year. I miss them greatly.

Charlotte, my sister, was the oldest child of the second set of children fathered by my father. Attractive and friendly, she was fun-loving, sentimental, and easy with people. She was married to Louis Carter, a devoted man, and the couple produced six children. I'm particularly grateful to her, because she took care of my mother during her final days. She was a patient, loving caregiver who tried to meet every one of my mama's needs until the end.

On June 15, 2003, Charlotte rode with one of her sons to visit our sister, Wilhelmenia, who was in a Washington, D.C., hospital with breast cancer. Charlotte stayed a couple of days with her daughter, Mary Ann, who lives here. Her daughter said it was one of the most wonderful times she ever had with her mother. I met her at the hospital just before she was about to leave to go back. She wrapped her arms around me as if she didn't want to let me go. I didn't know that would be the last time I would see her.

The next day after Charlotte got home in South Carolina, her husband found her on the floor and frantically called for an ambulance. She was rushed to the hospital and later died. She passed away on June 21, 2003, of a massive heart attack. God rest her soul.

The second soul I want to mention is Wilhelmenia Bowman Bennett, my beloved sister. She came to Washington in the early 1960s to enroll in college, Minor Teachers College, and was happy to live with me. We really got along very well. In fact, when I met Elaine, I was living with my sister, who took to my sweetheart right away. Wilhelmenia, after some determination and bitter tears, left her childhood beau, Robert (Bobby) Bennett, back home in South Carolina, but her heart could not take being away from him for too long. After she was in the city for about a year, Bobby came here and got a job at Ottenberg's Bakery. It was not long before these lovebirds announced wedding plans. Completely devoted to her, Bobby worked extra hours so she could finish school, earning a degree in education and a teaching job in the city's public schools. Later, she earned a master's degree in education.

Unfortunately, Wilhelmenia developed breast cancer in the late 1990s. She did not let the disease get her down, and she enjoyed ten productive years after her dreadful diagnosis. On April 24, 2005, Wilhelmenia passed away from cancer, surrounded by her loved ones.

Lastly, Robert was my model, my mentor, and my favorite. I remember the sadness when he left home early and joined the Marines. I also recall how his uniform just filled me with admiration as he stood on the porch and saluted me. When he came home from basic training, he sought out his darling, Albertha, a local girl from Sumter, South Carolina, and married her. They wasted no time, departing home for the big city, New York City. They had two children. A faithful employee, Robert drove a city bus for forty years. Upon his retirement, the couple moved back to Sumter to spend their retirement years around family and friends.

Everybody loved Robert, for he was a loyal friend, open-minded, and honest. He was never too busy to come to your rescue. Elaine says Robert reminded her of me—just a very nice man with a big, big heart. She also says we looked just alike but I don't know about that. I think he was more handsome. You could see the love he had for his wife each and every time they went out. They enjoyed going to church—the singing, the sermons—and going out for an occasional dinner.

Albertha, his wife, was an excellent cook and served many meals for us when we visited them. We used to go there every holiday and two or three times during the summer. Suddenly, Albertha was stricken with cancer and Robert took his caregiver duties in stride, waiting on her lovingly. But a year passed and then she died. Heartsick and totally depressed, Robert seemed not to want to live anymore. His health began to fail and diabetes seemed to overtake him.

We buried Robert on September 13, 2007, in a plot next to his beloved wife, Albertha. Although I knew he was going to die, I was still unprepared for it. Death is absolutely frightening, the unknown final destination. I never liked the notion of death. It has always made me uncomfortable, but it is a part of life. In a fleeting moment at his funeral, I thought back to the time when Senator Maybank died and how deeply it affected me. It shook me for weeks.

Yes, death is a bitter pill to swallow. For the last five months of Robert's life, I traveled to South Carolina every two weeks to see him. Sometimes Elaine could not go with me but I was faithful in being at his bedside. Often I would take a plane from the city to Columbia, South Carolina, and then rent a car to drive the long sixty miles to see my brother. That was how much he meant to me.

I guess it must have been the last Super Bowl game we watched together, the 2007 one, and he was home from the hospital. We had a very good time there. We spent the entire day together, watching the game, talking about the good days in Summerton, and eating fried chicken. Neither one of us was supposed to eat it. Our diets prohibited it. Once you got him started, Robert could talk up a streak, talked your ear off. I loved to see him in good spirits. You know how I feel about the Fourth of July—that is my holiday. On the Fourth of July of 2007, I visited Robert, and sat and talked with him about the family, the South, sports, women, and just life in general. He was in a lot of pain but his mind was still clear. Sometimes he remembered things that had long escaped my memory.

Today, I remember all of the things we discussed, how life can be so fleeting, how obstacles and challenges fall by the wayside, and how joy and peace of mind are sometimes all that matters. To be honest, Robert was a very wise man. He made me feel so grateful that I live in a great country where hard work and determination can spell success. He made me feel grateful that I had work that I enjoyed and the family and friends that I had. He made me feel grateful that I loved and married such a wonderful, caring woman. He made me grateful that I am alive.

IN A TIME when so many things come with a helping of intolerance and evil, I know that the example of my life is probably a beacon against bigotry, hate, and second-class citizenship. I had a chance to get bogged down by my past and the region in which I lived, but I decided to seize control of my life. I felt hemmed in, trapped, and penciled in as a statistic. I didn't want to be any of those things. When I ran away from Summerton, I voted with my feet and chose a freedom for my life that the South would have denied me at that time. I had dreams but I kept focused on the small steps, one at a time.

By taking the road to an uncertain future, I knew I had to be bold, courageous, and take risks if I was to have a better life. I refused to be resentful of people who had more than me. I refused to give up and settle for less. I acknowledged what I had, what my ancestors and my elders had given me, and chose to build on this legacy. I learned how to make something out of nothing. I believed in myself.

I have a good life and as long as God sees fit, I will continue to live it step by step.

Life Lessons

S OME OF US ELDERS are scratching our heads, trying to figure out what went wrong with today's youth. Supposedly Jim Crow was dead, so everything was going to get better. Our progress and achievements soared after the end of the civil rights movement, but later they went into a tailspin, and seemed to vanish for many like steam on a warm window pane. Our youngsters have picked up some of the worst habits in America. Truthfully, our young folks didn't used to act like this. We must realize that some of them have not been allowed to be kids during their brief lives. They have been treated as if they were grown-ups, and have never been wanted or loved. Some of them think we will turn away if they reach out.

We, as their elders, must stand by them, encouraging and supporting them. We can help them surpass the dreams and ambitions of their parents. It would be a sin to abandon them now, when they need us so much. We cannot neglect them. We must make the time to rescue them. When I was writing this book, our young people were very much on my mind. Like many in my generation, I'm worried about them. Although I grew up in a very different era, as I made my way through life I learned many lessons whose worth was the same in that time as in this modern time. Some of it is mother wit; some of it is common sense. It is important to pass these lessons on.

- You can take pride in any work, so long as you do it well. No task is too big or too small.
- Always be truthful with yourself. Not only talk the truth, think the truth.
- No achievement comes without sacrifice and discipline.
- Be trustworthy and dependable. Keep focused. Think before you speak. Find good role models and learn from them.
- College is a good thing, but it is not for everyone. You can be successful without a degree.
- Admit when you are wrong, correct the mistake, say you are sorry, and move on. Admit when you don't understand something.
- Don't get excited over titles. It is not what you are called but how you accept the calling.
- Nevertheless, if you are in the company of important people, learn the expected protocol and be respectful.
- Don't carry grudges or bad feelings. Be forgiving of yourself and others.
- Make a plan. Never go for the quick fix or the easy way. Every goal requires hard work, courage, and determination.
- Remember that life is not all about you. Other people matter. Smile.
- There is no reason to be bored. Find the joy, the pleasure, in little things.
- Live in the glow of today and not in the pain of the past.
- Value the relationships you make. Be kind and helpful to

those with whom you work. One might grow up to be president.

And a final caveat: Running away to start a new life at age thirteen may have been good for Bertie Bowman in 1944, but I do not recommend it for any child in these different times!

⊷⊜ ACKNOWLEDGMENTS ⊜⊷

I never thought it would happen. When I first started sharing my life story with my wife, Elaine, she insisted on recording and writing down all of the details. And she hasn't stopped since. Her influence is found in every phase of this project and on every page of this book, from the first transcription of a recorded story to the final words and sentences that appear in print. To put it honestly, it starts—and ends—with Elaine, and my gratitude to her goes beyond simple acknowledgment. We are partners in life and in this venture.

When I first found out that I would have space in this book to thank people who helped me with this project, I was tempted to list everyone who ever said a kind word to me in my seventy-seven years in this world. However, I will try to restrain myself and cut short my long list. So, if you helped in this process and you don't see your name, please know that I am no less grateful for your help.

Foremost on my list are my sisters, Annie House and Dorothy Floyd, my brothers, Larry and Jimmy Lee Bowman and my brother-in-law, Robert (Bobby) Bennett. They were invaluable sounding boards for me during this process.

I would not have had the courage to undertake or complete this book without the love and support of my children LaUanah and Ted Cassell. Their detailed and painstaking audits were priceless.

Special gratitude is owed my very dear friends Walt and Marge Wolfram, who encouraged me over thirty years ago to record my life story. I would never have discovered that I lived a life that someone would want to read about if Walt and Marge had not been a part of it.

Another friend to whom I owe enormous thanks is the architect of my proposal, Linda Cashdan. Together, she and Elaine produced a document that made many people say, "I could not put it down." Throughout the long process of firming the chapters, Linda and her husband, Dave, drilled me between innings as we cheered on our beloved Nationals baseball team.

Thanks are due to to my agent, Scott Mendel, who never wavered in his belief in me and this book. Thanks, Scott, for taking a chance on it and for being a voice of reassurance.

I am also honored to have a brilliant editor, Melody Guy, who loved my life story right away and moved quickly to sell it to her superiors at Ballantine.

While pushing forward in this venture, I met Robert Fleming, whose imprint in this book is indelible and transparent. He worked very hard with Elaine and me to give the manuscript the flavor it most definitely needed.

I have accomplished little in my thirty-plus years on the Senate Foreign Relations Committee without the guidance of our director of protocol, Sandra Mason. This book was no exception. Thanks, Sandy.

I also appreciate the support from my South Carolina friends Leon Watson, Joe Butler, and Joe Robinson and my longtime friend, Oscar Quarles.

I owe an enormous debt of gratitude to the chief clerk of the Senate Foreign Relations Committee, Susan Oursler, and our deputy chief, Megan Moyerman, for standing in for me and supporting me all the way.

Thanks to the Senate Federal Credit Union for graciously allowing me to use the boardroom for the book markup. Special thanks to the CEO, Susan Enis, and the very able meeting coordinator, Patti Lingafelt.

My respect for libraries and librarians increased immensely while I was working on this book. Elaine dragged me from the Clarendon County Archives and the Harvin Clarendon County Library in Manning, South Carolina, through the Library of Congress, and to the shelves of the Senate Documents Room. Special thanks to Janet Meleney, Archivist, Emma Hilton, Librarian, and Barbara Thomas, Senate Document Clerk, for their help.

My hearty thanks also goes to Patsy Fletcher of the D.C. Historic Preservation Office for helping Elaine and me understand the historic value of my life story.

I cannot end this journey without thanking my computer teacher, Earl Thomas Jr. When I began this work, neither Elaine or I had ever set a finger on a computer and never planned to do so at our age. Although I am still not having fun with it, "Junior" got me here and I am truly grateful to him.

Many friends have supported me with a bountiful supply of prayers, and I am certain that I could not have finished this book without the serenity I drew from those prayers.

In the infant stages of this project, God took my father-in-law and business partner, Earl E. King Sr. home to be with him. I missed his input, but it was counterbalanced by the pleasure of having my mother-in-law, Elizabeth King, live with us for twelve years. She kept me company many nights as I worked on this book.

Finally, I must mention that some of the happiness that fills my heart today is diminished. While I struggled to finish this book, two sisters, Charlotte Carter and Wilhelmenia Bennett and my dear brother Robert, went home to be with the Lord. They were in my thoughts constantly as I recalled my childhood but I am all right with it because I know they are in a better place.

ABOUT THE AUTHOR

BERTIE BOWMAN has served as hearing coordinator for the
Senate Foreign Relations Committee since 2000, when the
executive appointment of then committee chairman Jesse
Helms brought him back to the Senate after a ten-year
hiatus. Before his retirement in 1990, Bertie Bowman had
worked for the Foreign Relations Committee for twenty-five
years, first as committee clerk and then as assistant hearing
coordinator. He owns and operates Bertie's Limousine Service, a chauffeur company that provides services for Washington VIPs, foreign diplomats, and others in and around
the metropolitan D.C. area. Bowman is an elected member
of the board of directors of the Senate Federal Credit Union,
a member of the D.C. Board of Funeral Directors, and is
active in many community volunteer organizations.

ABOUT THE TYPE

This book is set in Simoncini Garamond. Some of the most popular typefaces in history are those based on the types of the sixteenth-century printer, publisher, and type designer Claude Garamond, whose sixteenth-century types were modeled on those of Venetian printers from the end of the previous century. Later typefaces by Jean Jannon in the early 1600s were long wrongly attributed to Garamond. Between 1958 and 1961, the Italian foundry Simoncini issued its version of Garamond (actually based on Jannon's typefaces), designed by Francesco Simoncini and W. Bilz. More delicate in line and lighter in color than other Garamond/Jannon inspired typefaces, Simoncini Garamond is very versatile in display as well as text situations.